The Power of a
PRAYING®
WIFE

STORMIE
OMARTIAN

HARVEST HOUSE PUBLISHERS

EUGENE, OREGON

Cover by Koechel Peterson & Associates, Minneapolis, Minnesota

THE POWER OF A PRAYING® WIFE

Copyright © 1997 by Stormie Omartian
Eugene, Oregon 97402
www.harvesthousepublishers.com

The Library of Congress has cataloged the edition as follows:

Omartian, Stormie.
   The power of a praying wife / Stormie Omartian.
      p.   cm.

Trade Edition	Deluxe Edition
ISBN-13: 978-0-7369-1924-1	ISBN-13: 978-0-7369-0600-5
ISBN-10: 0-7369-1924-4	ISBN-10: 0-7369-0600-2

   1. Wives—Religious life.   2. Intercessory prayer—Christianity.
I. Title.
BV4527.043   1997   97-7436
248.8'435—dc21   CIP

Printed in the United States of America

07 08 09 10 11 12 13 14 15 / BP / 14 13 12 11 10 9 8 7 6 5 4 3 2 1

This book is dedicated with love to my husband, Michael, who has consistently given me more than I ever wanted to pray about. You and I both know that prayer works.

Contents

Foreword

The Power................................... 13

1. His Wife 25

2. His Work................................. 49

3. His Finances 55

4. His Sexuality............................. 61

5. His Affection............................. 69

6. His Temptations 75

7. His Mind................................. 81

8. His Fears 87

9. His Purpose 93

10. His Choices.............................. 99

11. His Health.............................. 103

12. His Protection.......................... 107

13. His Trials............................... 111

14. His Integrity 117

15. His Reputation 121

16. His Priorities........................... 127

17. His Relationships....................... 131

18. His Fatherhood 137

19. His Past................................ 143

20. His Attitude 149

21. His Marriage 153

22. His Emotions. 159
23. His Walk 163
24. His Talk. 169
25. His Repentance 173
26. His Deliverance. 177
27. His Obedience. 183
28. His Self-Image 189
29. His Faith 195
30. His Future 199

Acknowledgments

With special thanks:

✍ To my secretary, Susan Martinez, for bearing the load of another book deadline. Your love as a sister, faithfulness as a friend, and richness as a prayer partner can only be equaled by your efficiency and dedication as my highly treasured and irreplaceable assistant.

✍ To my prayer partners and fellow praying wives, Sally Anderson, Susan Martinez, Donna Summer, Katie Stewart, Roz Thompson, and Jan Williamson, who have experienced along with me what gut-level, crying-out-to-God intercession for our husbands really means. Without your deep and faithful commitment to God and to prayer, this book might never have been written. You are eternal treasures in my heart.

✍ To my daughter, Mandy, and my son, Chris, for loving your dad and me, even through the times we didn't model for you the best way to run a marriage. I regret any time we argued in front of you, before we learned that prayer is more powerful than contention. I pray that you will carry all the good we have learned into your own marriages.

✍ To my new son, John David Kendrick, for letting me be your mom on earth now that your dad is in heaven with your mom. You are what our family has been missing all these years and we didn't know it until you came to be with us.

✍ To Pastor Jack and Anna Hayford, and Pastor Dale and Joan Evrist for teaching me how to pray and showing me the way a good marriage works.

✍ To my Harvest House family, Bob Hawkins Sr., Bob Hawkins Jr., Bill Jensen, Julie McKinney, Teresa Evenson, Betty Fletcher, and LaRae Weikert for your enthusiasm about the book and your consistently positive input. You are all a delight. And to Editorial Director Carolyn McCready for being such a joy. Thank you for your encouragement.

✍ To my editor, Holly Halverson, for your good eye and sharp mind.

✍ To Tom and Patti Brussat, Michael and Terry Harriton, Jan and Dave Williamson, and Dave and Priscilla Navarro for sharing your lives and experiences in order to give me good examples of the power of a praying wife.

Foreword

There is a joke in our household when I refer to the number of years Stormie and I have been married. I always say, "It's been twenty-five wonderful years for me and twenty-five miserable years for her." After twenty-five years of marriage to Stormie, there aren't any phases of my complex personality left for her to discover. She has seen me triumph, fail, struggle, be fearful and depressed, and doubt my competency as a husband, father, and musician. She has seen me angry at God because He wouldn't jump when I asked Him to. She has witnessed miracles, as God redeemed something from the ashes to gold. Every step of the way has been accompanied by her prayers and this book was written from her experience over the years. I cannot imagine what my life would be without her praying for me. It gives me comfort and security, and also fulfills the mission the Lord has for us to pray for each other and bear one another's burdens. I can think of no better way to truly love your husband than by lifting him up in prayer on a consistent basis. It is a priceless gift that helps him experience God's blessings and grace.

Stormie, I love you.

Your covered-in-prayer husband,
Michael

Who can find a virtuous wife? For her worth is far above rubies. The heart of her husband safely trusts her; so he will have no lack of gain. She does him good and not evil all the days of her life.
PROVERBS 31:10-12

The Power

First of all, let me make it perfectly clear that the power of a praying wife is not a means of gaining control over your husband, so don't get your hopes up! In fact, it is quite the opposite. It's laying down all claim to power in and of yourself, and relying on God's power to transform you, your husband, your circumstances, and your marriage. This power is not given to wield like a weapon in order to beat back an unruly beast. It's a gentle tool of restoration appropriated through the prayers of a wife who longs to *do* right more than *be* right, and to *give life* more than *get even*. It's a way to invite God's power into your husband's life for his greatest blessing, which is ultimately yours, too.

When my husband, Michael, and I were first married and differences arose between us, praying was definitely not my first thought. In fact, it was closer to a last resort. I tried other methods first such as arguing, pleading, ignoring, avoiding, confronting, debating, and of course the ever-popular silent treatment, all with far less than satisfying results. It took some time to realize that by praying *first*, these unpleasant methods of operation could be avoided.

By the time you read this book, Michael and I will have been married over a quarter of a century. This is nothing less than miraculous. It's certainly not a testimony to our greatness, but to God's faithfulness to answer prayer. I confess that even after all these years, I am still learning about this and it doesn't come easy. While I may not have as much practice doing it right as I have had doing it wrong, I can say without reservation that *prayer works*.

Unfortunately, I didn't learn how to *really* pray for my husband until I started praying for my children. As I saw profound answers to prayer for them, I decided to try being just as detailed and fervent in praying for him. But I found that praying for children is far easier. From the first moment we lay eyes on them, we want the best for their lives—unconditionally, wholeheartedly, without question. But with a husband, it's often not that simple—especially for someone who's been married awhile. A husband can hurt your feelings, be inconsiderate, uncaring, abusive, irritating, or negligent. He can say or do things that pierce your heart like a sliver. And every time you start to pray for him, you find the sliver festering. It's obvious you can't give yourself to praying the way God wants you to until you are rid of it.

Praying for your husband is not the same as praying for a child (even though it may seem similar), because you are not your husband's mother. We have authority over our children that is given to us by the Lord. We *don't* have authority over our husbands. However, we have been given authority "over all the power of the enemy" (Luke 10:19) and can do great damage to the enemy's plans when we pray. Many difficult things that happen in a marriage relationship are actually part of the enemy's plan set up for its demise. But we can say, "I will not allow anything to destroy my marriage."

"I will not stand by and watch my husband be wearied, beaten down, or destroyed."

"I will not sit idle while an invisible wall goes up between us."

"I will not allow confusion, miscommunication, wrong attitudes, and bad choices to erode what we are trying to build together."

"I will not tolerate hurt and unforgiveness leading us to divorce." We can take a stand against any negative influences in our marriage relationship and know that God has given us authority in His name to back it up.

You have the means to establish a hedge of protection around your marriage because Jesus said, "Whatever you bind on earth will be bound in heaven, and whatever you loose on earth will be loosed in heaven" (Matthew 18:18). You have authority in the name of Jesus to *stop evil* and *permit good.* You can submit to God in prayer whatever controls your husband—alcoholism, workaholism, laziness, depression, infirmity, abusiveness, anxiety, fear, or failure—and pray for him to be released from it.

Wait! Before You Write Off the Marriage . . . . .

I confess right now that there was a time when I considered separation or divorce. This is an embarrassing disclosure because I don't believe either of those options is the best answer to a troubled marriage. I believe in God's position on divorce. He says it's not right and it grieves Him. The last thing I want to do is grieve God. But I know what it's like to feel the kind of despair that paralyzes good decision making. I've experienced the degree of hopelessness that causes a person to give up on trying to do what's right. I understand the torture of loneliness that leaves you longing for anyone who will look into your soul and see *you.*

I've felt pain so bad that the fear of dying from it propelled me to seek out the only immediately foreseeable means of survival: escape from the source of agony. I know what it's like to contemplate acts of desperation because you see no future. I've experienced such a buildup of negative emotions day after day that separation and divorce seemed like nothing more than the promise of pleasant relief.

The biggest problem I faced in our marriage was my husband's temper. The only ones who were ever the object of his anger were me and the children. He used words like weapons that left me crippled or paralyzed. I'm not saying that I was without fault—quite the contrary. I was sure I was as much to blame as he, but I didn't know what to do about it. I pleaded with God on a regular basis to make my husband more sensitive, less angry, more pleasant, less irritable. But I saw few changes. Was God not listening? Or did He favor the husband over the wife, as I suspected?

After a number of years, with little change, I cried out to the Lord one day in despair, saying, "God, I can't live this way anymore. I know what You've said about divorce, but I can't live in the same house with him. Help me, Lord." I sat on the bed holding my Bible for hours as I struggled with the strongest desire to take the children and leave. I believe that because I came to God in total honesty about what I felt, He allowed me to thoroughly and clearly envision what life would be like if I left: Where I would live, how I would support myself and care for the children, who would still be my friends, and worst of all, how a heritage of divorce would affect my son and daughter. It was the most horrible and unspeakably sad picture. If I left I would find some relief, but at the price of everything dear to me. I knew it wasn't God's plan for us.

As I sat there, God also impressed upon my heart that if I would deliberately lay down my life before His throne, die to the desire to leave, and give my needs to Him, He would teach me how to lay down my life in prayer for Michael. He would show me how to really intercede for him as a son of God, and in the process He would revive my marriage and pour His blessings out on both of us. We would be better together, if we could get past this, than we could ever be separated and alone. He showed me that Michael was caught in a web from his past that rendered him incapable of being different from what he was at that moment, but God would use me as an instrument of His deliverance if I would consent to it. It hurt to say yes to this and I cried a lot. But when I did, I felt hopeful for the first time in years.

I began to pray every day for Michael, like I had never prayed before. Each time, though, I had to confess my own hardness of heart. I saw how deeply hurt and unforgiving of him I was. *I don't want to pray for him. I don't want to ask God to bless him. I only want God to strike his heart with lightning and convict him of how cruel he has been*, I thought. I had to say over and over, "God, I confess my unforgiveness toward my husband. Deliver me from all of it."

Little by little, I began to see changes occur in both of us. When Michael became angry, instead of reacting negatively, I prayed for him. I asked God to give me insight into what was causing his rage. He did. I asked Him what I could do to make things better. He showed me. My husband's anger became less frequent and more quickly soothed. Every day, prayer built something positive. We're still not perfected, but we've come a long way. It hasn't been easy, yet I'm convinced that God's way is worth the effort it takes to walk in it. It's the only way to save a marriage.

A wife's prayers for her husband have a far greater effect on him than anyone else's, even his mother's. (Sorry, Mom.) A mother's prayers for her child are certainly fervent. But when a man marries, he leaves his father and mother and becomes one with his wife (Matthew 19:5). They are a team, one unit, unified in spirit. The strength of a man and wife joined together in God's sight is *far* greater than the sum of the strengths of each of the two individuals. That's because the Holy Spirit unites them and gives added power to their prayers.

That's also why there is so much at stake if we *don't* pray. Can you imagine praying for the right side of your body and not the left? If the right side is not sustained and protected and it falls, it's going to bring down the left side with it. The same is true of you and your husband. If you pray for yourself and not him, you will never find the blessings and fulfillment you want. What happens to him happens to you and you can't get around it.

This oneness gives us a power that the enemy doesn't like. That's why he devises ways to weaken it. He gives us whatever we will fall for, whether it be low self-esteem, pride, the need to be right, miscommunication, or the bowing to our own selfish desires. He will tell you lies like, "Nothing will ever change." "Your failures are irreparable." "There's no hope for reconciliation." "You'd be happier with someone else." He'll tell you whatever you will believe, because he knows if he can get you to believe it, there is no future for your marriage. If you believe enough lies, your heart will eventually be hardened against God's truth.

In every broken marriage, there is at least one person whose heart is hard against God. When a heart becomes hard, there is no vision from God's perspective. When we're miserable in a marriage, we feel that anything will be an improvement over what we're experiencing. But we don't see the whole picture. We only see the way it is, not the way God wants it to become. When we pray, however, our hearts become *soft* toward God and we get a vision. We see there is

hope. We have faith that He will restore all that has been devoured, destroyed, and eaten away from the marriage. "I will
restore to you the years that the swarming locust has eaten"
(Joel 2:25). We can trust Him to take away the pain, hopelessness, hardness, and unforgiveness. We are able to envision
His ability to resurrect love and life from the deadest of places.

Imagine Mary Magdalene's joy when she went to Jesus'
tomb the third day after He had been crucified and found
that He was not dead after all, but had been raised up by the
power of God. The joy of seeing something hopelessly dead
brought to life is the greatest joy we can know. The power
that resurrected Jesus is the very same power that will resurrect the dead places of your marriage and put life back
into it. "God both raised up the Lord and will also raise us
up by His power" (1 Corinthians 6:14). It's the only power
that can. But it doesn't happen without a heart for God that
is willing to gut it out in prayer, grow through tough times,
and wait for love to be resurrected. We have to go through
the pain to get to the joy.

You have to decide if you want your marriage to work,
and if you want it badly enough to do whatever is necessary,
within healthy parameters, to see it happen. *You* have to believe the part of your relationship that has been eaten away
by pain, indifference, and selfishness can be restored. *You*
have to trust that what has swarmed over you, such as abuse,
death of a child, infidelity, poverty, loss, catastrophic illness,
or accident, can be relieved of its death grip. *You* have to determine that everything consuming you and your husband,
such as workaholism, alcoholism, drug abuse, or depression,
can be destroyed. *You* have to know that whatever has crept
into your relationship so silently and stealthily as to not
even be perceived as a threat until it is clearly present—
such as making idols of your career, your dreams, your kids,

or your selfish desires—can be removed. You have to trust that God is big enough to accomplish all this and more.

If you wake up one morning with a stranger in your bed and it's your husband, if you experience a silent withdrawal from one another's lives that severs all emotional connection, if you sense a relentless draining away of love and hope, if your relationship is in so bottomless a pit of hurt and anger that every day sends you deeper into despair, if every word spoken drives a wedge further between you until it becomes an impenetrable barrier keeping you miles apart, be assured that none of the above is God's will for your marriage. God's will is to break down all these barriers and lift you out of that pit. He can heal the wounds and put love back in your heart. Nothing and no one else can.

But you have to rise up and say, "Lord, I pray for an end to this conflict and a breaking of the hold strife has on us. Take away the hurt and the armor we've put up to protect ourselves. Lift us out of the pit of unforgiveness. Speak through us so that our words reflect Your love, peace, and reconciliation. Tear down this wall between us and teach us how to walk through it. Enable us to rise up from this paralysis and move into the healing and wholeness You have for us."

Don't write off the marriage. Ask God to give you a new husband. He is able to take the one you have and make him a new creation in Christ. Husbands and wives are not destined to fight, emotionally disconnect, live in marital deadness, be miserable, or divorce. We have God's power on our side. We don't have to leave our marriages to chance. We can fight for them in prayer and not give up, because as long as we are praying, there is hope. With God, nothing is ever as dead as it seems. Not even your own feelings.

What About Me? I Need Prayer, Too.

It's natural to enter into this prayer venture wondering if your husband will ever be praying for you in the same way you're praying for him. While that would certainly be great, don't count on it. Praying for your husband will be an act of unselfish, unconditional love and sacrifice on your part. You must be willing to make this commitment knowing it is quite possible—even highly probable—that he will never pray for you in the same way. In some cases, he may not pray for you at all. You can ask him to, and you can pray for him to pray for you, but you can't demand it of him. Regardless, whether he does or doesn't is not your concern, it's God's. So release him from that obligation. If he doesn't pray for you, it's *his* loss more than yours anyway. Your happiness and fulfillment will not ride on whether he prays, it will depend on your own relationship with the Lord. Yes, wives need prayer, too. But I'm convinced we should not depend on our husbands to be the sole providers of it. In fact, looking to your husband to be your dedicated prayer partner could be a setup for failure and disappointment for both of you.

I learned that the best thing for our marriage was for me to have women prayer partners with whom I prayed every week. I now believe this is vital for any marriage. If you can find two or more strong, faith-filled women whom you thoroughly trust, and with whom you can share the longings of your heart, set up a weekly prayer time. It will change your life. This doesn't mean you have to tell your prayer partners everything about your husband or expose the private details of his life. The purpose is to ask God to make *your* heart right, show *you* how to be a good wife, share the burdens of *your* soul, and seek God's blessing on your husband.

Of course, if there is an issue with serious consequences, and you can trust your prayer partners with the confidential nature of your request, by all means share it. I've seen many marriages end in separation or divorce because people were too prideful or afraid to share their problems with someone who could pray for them. They go along putting up a good front and suddenly one day the marriage is over. Be sure to stress the confidential nature of what you're sharing with your prayer partners, but don't throw away the marriage because you're hesitant to pray about it with others. If you have a prayer partner who can't keep a confidence, find someone else with more wisdom, sensitivity, and spiritual maturity.

Even without prayer partners or a praying husband, when you pray fervently you'll see things happen. *Before* your prayers are answered there will be blessings from God that will come to you simply because you are praying. That's because you will have spent time in the presence of God, where all lasting transformation begins.

One Prayer at a Time

Don't be overwhelmed by the many ways there are to pray for your husband. It's not necessary to do it all in one day, one week, or even a month. Let the suggestions in this book be a guide and then pray as the Holy Spirit leads you. Where there are tough issues and you need a dynamic breakthrough, fasting will make your prayers more effective. Also, praying Scripture over your husband is powerful. That's what I have done in the prayers at the end of each chapter, wherever you see a Scripture reference.

Above all, don't give place to impatience. Seeing answers to your prayers can take time, especially if your marriage is deeply wounded or strained. Be patient to persevere and wait for God to heal. Keep in mind that you are both imperfect people. Only the Lord is perfect. Look to God as the source of all you want to see happen in your marriage, and don't worry about *how* it will happen. It's your responsibility to pray. It's God's job to answer. Leave it in *His* hands.

CHAPTER ONE

His Wife

The hard part about being a praying wife, other than the sacrifice of time, is maintaining a pure heart. It must be clean before God in order for you to see good results. That's why praying for a husband must begin with praying for his wife. If you have resentment, anger, unforgiveness, or an ungodly attitude, even if there's good reason for it, you'll have a difficult time seeing answers to your prayers. But if you can release those feelings to God in total honesty and then move into prayer, there is nothing that can change a marriage more dramatically. Sometimes wives sabotage their own prayers because they don't pray them from a right heart. It took me awhile to figure that out.

My Favorite Three-word Prayer

I wish I could say that I've been regularly praying for my husband from the beginning of our marriage until now. I haven't. At least not like I'm suggesting in this book. Oh, I prayed. The prayers were short: "Protect him, Lord." They were to the point: "Save our marriage." But most commonly they were my favorite three-word prayer: "Change him, Lord."

When we were first married, I was a new believer coming out of a life of great bondage and error and had much to learn about the delivering and restoring power of God. I thought I had married a man who was close to perfect, and what wasn't perfect was cute. As time went on, cute became irritating and perfect became driving perfectionism. I decided that what irritated me most about him had to be changed and then everything would be fine.

It took a number of years for me to realize my husband was never going to conform to my image. It took a few years beyond that to understand I couldn't make him change in *any* way. In fact, it wasn't until I started going to God with what bothered me that I began to see any difference at all. And then it didn't happen the way I thought it would. *I* was the one God worked on first. *I* was the one who began to change. My heart had to be softened, humbled, pummeled, molded, and reconstructed before He even started working on my husband. *I* had to learn to see things according to the way God saw them—not how I thought they should be.

Gradually I realized it's impossible to truly give yourself in prayer for your husband without first examining your own heart. I couldn't go to God and expect answers to prayer if I harbored unforgiveness, bitterness, or resentment. I couldn't pray *my* favorite three-word prayer without knowing in the deepest recesses of my soul that I had to first pray *God's* favorite three-word prayer: "Change me, Lord."

Who, Me? . . . Change?

Don't say I didn't warn you. When you pray for your husband, especially in the hopes of changing him, you can surely expect some changes. But the first changes won't be in *him*. They'll be in *you*. If this makes you as mad as it made me, you'll say, "Wait a minute! I'm not the one that needs changing here!" But God sees things we don't. He knows where we have room for improvement. He doesn't have to search long to uncover attitudes and habits that are outside His perfect will for us. He requires us to not sin in our hearts because sin separates us from Him and we don't get our prayers answered. "If I regard iniquity in my heart, the Lord will not hear" (Psalm 66:18). God wants our hearts to be right so the answers to our prayers are not compromised.

This whole requirement is especially hard when you feel your husband has sinned against you with unkindness, lack of respect, indifference, irresponsibility, infidelity, abandonment, cruelty, or abuse. But God considers the sins of unforgiveness, anger, hatred, self-pity, lovelessness, and revenge to be just as bad as any others. Confess them and ask God to set you free from anything that is not of Him. One of the greatest gifts you can give your husband is your own wholeness. The most effective tool in transforming him may be your own transformation.

Don't worry, I struggled with all this, too. In fact, every time my husband and I came to an impasse, God and I had a conversation that went something like this:

"Do you see the way he is, Lord?"
"Do you see the way *you* are?"
"Lord, are You saying there are things you want to change in me?"
"Many things. Are you ready to hear them?"
"Well, I guess so."
"Tell me when you're really ready."
"Why me, God? *He's* the one that needs to change."
"The point is not who *needs* to change. The point is who is *willing* to change."
"But God, this isn't fair."
"I never said life is fair, I said *I* am fair."

"But I . . ."

"Someone has to be willing to start."

"But. . . ."

"How important is preserving your marriage?"

"Very important. The other options are unacceptable."

"I rest my case. Let's get on with changing you."

"Help me to have a good attitude about this, Lord."

"That's up to you."

"Do I have to pray for my husband even if he's not praying for me?"

"Precisely."

"But that's not . . . okay, okay, I remember. Life's not fair. *You're* fair!"

(Silent nodding from heaven)

"I give up. Go ahead. Oh, this is going to be painful! Cha . . . change. . . . I can't believe I'm saying this."

(Deep breath) "Change me, Lord."

Painful? Yes! Dying to yourself is always painful. Especially when you are convinced that the other person needs more changing than you. But this kind of pain leads to *life*. The other alternative is just as painful and its ultimate end is the death of a dream, a relationship, a marriage, and a family.

God can resurrect the deadest of marriages, but it takes humbling ourselves before Him and desiring to live His way— forgiveness, kindness, and love. It means letting go of the past and all hurt associated with it and being willing to lose the argument in order to win the battle. I'm not saying you have to become a person void of personality, feelings, or thoughts of your own, or be the whipping post for a husband's whim. God doesn't require that of you. (In fact, if you are in any kind of physical or emotional danger, remove yourself immediately from the situation to a place of safety and get help. You can pray from there while your husband receives the counseling he needs.) Submission is something you give from your heart, not something demanded of you. Jesus said, "He who loses his life for My sake will find it" (Matthew 10:39). But laying down your life is something you willingly do, *not* something that is forcefully taken from you. What I'm saying is that your attitude must be, "Whatever You want, Lord. Show me and I'll do it." It means being willing to die to yourself and say, "Change me, Lord."

The Ultimate Love Language

Something amazing happens to our hearts when we pray for another person. The hardness melts. We become able to get beyond the hurts, and forgive. We even end up loving the person we are praying for. It's miraculous! It happens because when we pray we enter into the presence of God and He fills us with His Spirit of love. When you pray for your husband, the love of God will grow in your heart for him. Not only that, you'll find love growing in *his* heart for *you*, without him even knowing you are praying. That's because prayer is the ultimate love language. It communicates in ways we can't. I've seen women with no feelings of love for their husbands find that as they prayed, over time, those feelings came. Sometimes they felt differently even after the first heartfelt prayer.

Talking to God about your husband is an act of love. Prayer gives rise to love, love begets more prayer, which in turn gives rise to more love. Even if your praying is not born out of completely selfless motives, your motives will become more unselfish as prayer continues. You'll find yourself more loving in your responses. You'll notice that issues which formerly caused strife between you will no longer do that. You'll be able to come to mutual agreements without a fight. This unity is vital.

When we are not united, everything falls apart. Jesus said, "Every kingdom divided against itself is brought to desolation, and every city or house divided against itself will not stand" (Matthew 12:25). Prayer brings unity even if you aren't praying together. I've seen great tension relieved between my husband and me simply by praying for him. Also, asking him, "How can I pray for you?" brings an aspect of love and care into the situation. My husband will usually stop and answer that question in great detail when he might otherwise not say anything. I know of even nonbelieving husbands who respond positively to that question from their wives.

The point in all this is that as husband and wife we don't want to be taking separate roads. We want to be on the same path together. We want to be deeply compatible, lifelong companions, and have the love that lasts a lifetime. Prayer, as the ultimate love language, can make that happen.

I Don't Even Like Him—How Can I Pray for Him?

Have you ever been so mad at your husband that the last thing you wanted to do was pray for him? So have I. It's hard to pray for someone when you're angry or he's hurt you. But that's exactly what God wants us to do. If He asks us to pray for our *enemies*, how much more should we be praying for the person with whom we have become one and are supposed to love? But how do we get past the unforgiveness and critical attitude?

The first thing to do is be completely honest with God. In order to break down the walls in our hearts and smash the barriers that stop communication, we have to be totally up front with the Lord about our feelings. We don't have to "pretty it up" for Him. He already knows the truth. He just wants to see if we're willing to admit it and confess it as disobedience to His ways. If so, He then has a heart with which He can work.

If you are angry at your husband, tell God. Don't let it become a cancer that grows with each passing day. Don't say, "I'm going to live my life and let him live his." There's a price to pay when we act entirely independently of one another. "Neither is man independent of woman, nor woman independent of man, in the Lord" (1 Corinthians 11:11).

Instead say, "Lord, nothing in me wants to pray for this man. I confess my anger, hurt, unforgiveness, disappointment, resentment, and hardness of heart toward him. Forgive me and create in me a clean heart and right spirit before You. Give me a new, positive, joyful, loving, forgiving attitude toward him. Where he has erred, reveal it to him and convict his heart about it. Lead him through the paths of repentance and deliverance. Help me not to hold myself apart from him emotionally, mentally, or physically because of unforgiveness. Where either of us needs to ask forgiveness of the other, help us to do so. If there is something I'm not seeing that is adding to this problem, reveal it to me and help me to understand it. Remove any wedge of confusion that has created misunderstanding or miscommunication. Where there is behavior that needs to change in either of us, I pray You would enable that change to happen. As much as I want to hang on to my anger toward him because I feel it is justified, I want to do what *You* want. I release all those feelings to You. Give me a renewed sense of love for him and words to heal this situation."

If you feel you are able, try this little experiment and see what happens. Pray for your husband every day for a month using each one of the thirty areas of prayer focus I have included in this book. Pray a chapter a day. Ask God to pour out His blessings on him and fill you both with His love. See if your heart doesn't soften toward him. Notice if his attitude toward you doesn't change as well. Observe whether your relationship isn't running more smoothly. If you have trouble making that kind of prayer commitment, think of it from the Lord's perspective. Seeing your husband through God's eyes—not just as your husband, but as God's child, a son whom the Lord loves—can be a great revelation. If someone called and asked you to pray for his or her son, you would do it, wouldn't you? Well, God is asking.

"Shut Up and Pray"

There is a time for everything, it says in the Bible. And it is never more true than in a marriage, especially when it comes to the words we say. There is a time to speak and a time *not* to speak, and happy is the man whose wife can discern between the two. Anyone who has been married for any length of time realizes that there are things that are better left unsaid. A wife has the ability to hurt her husband more deeply than anyone else can, and he can do the same to her. No matter how much apology, the words can not be erased. They can only be forgiven and that is not always easy. Sometimes anything we say will only hinder the flow of what God wants to do, so it's best to, well, shut up and pray.

When Michael and I were first married, I didn't say much if I felt something was wrong. I stuffed my feelings inside. After our first child was born, I became increasingly vocal. But the more I voiced my objections and opinions, the more he resisted and the more we would argue. Whatever I said not only accomplished nothing in the area I wanted it to, it had the opposite effect. It took me a number of years to learn what millions of women have learned over the centuries. *Nagging doesn't work!* Criticizing doesn't work. Sometimes, just plain talking doesn't accomplish any-thing either. I've found that prayer is the only thing that *al-ways* works. The safeguard you have with prayer is that you have to go through God to do it. This means you can't get away with a bad attitude, wrong thinking, or incorrect mo-tives. When you pray, God reveals anything in your person-ality that is resistant to His order of things.

My husband will not do something he doesn't want to do. And if he ends up doing something he doesn't want to do, his immediate family members will pay for it. If there is anything I really want him to do, I've learned to pray about it until I have God's peace in my heart *before* I ask. Sometimes God changes my heart about it, or shows me a different way so I don't have to say anything. If I do need to say something, I try not to just blurt it out. I pray first for God's leading.

It took me a long time to figure this out, however. It hap-pened one day when I came across the Proverb, "Better to dwell in the wilderness, than with a contentious and angry woman" (Proverbs 21:19). For *some reason* it struck a nerve.

"But, Lord," I questioned, "what about 'Open rebuke is better than love carefully concealed' [Proverbs 27:5]? Don't we wives have to tell our husbands when something is wrong?"

He replied, "There is . . . a time for every purpose under heaven . . . a time to keep silence and a time to speak" (Ec-clesiastes 3:1,7). "The problem is you don't know when to do either. And you don't know how to do it in love."

"Okay, Lord," I said, "Show me when to speak and when to just keep quiet and pray."

The first opportunity for this came right away. I had started a new weekly women's prayer group in my home, and it was so life-changing I suggested to my husband that he start a similar group for men. But he wouldn't hear of it.

"I don't have time," was his not-too-pleased-at-the-idea answer.

The more I talked about it, the more irritated Michael became. After getting my "Be quiet and pray" directions from God, I decided to try that approach. I stopped talking about it and started praying. I also asked my prayer group to pray along with me. It was more than two years after I stopped mentioning it to him and started praying that Michael abruptly announced one day he was organizing a weekly men's prayer group. It has been going ever since, and he still doesn't know I prayed. Even though it took longer than I would have liked, it did happen. And there was peace in the waiting, which I wouldn't have had if I had not kept quiet.

Queen Esther in the Bible prayed, fasted, and sought God's timing before she approached her husband, the king, about a very important matter. There was a lot at stake and she knew it. She didn't run in and scream, "Your hoodlum friends are going to ruin our lives!" Rather she prayed first and then ministered to him in love, while God prepared his heart. The Lord will always give us words to say, and show us when to say them if we ask Him. Timing is everything.

I've known people who use the excuse of "just being honest" to devastate others with their words. The Bible says, "A fool vents all his feelings, but a wise man holds them back" (Proverbs 29:11). In other words, it's foolish to share every feeling and thought. Being honest doesn't mean you have to be completely frank in your every comment. That hurts people. While honesty is a requirement for a successful marriage, telling your husband everything that is wrong with him is not only ill-advised, it probably doesn't reveal the complete truth. The total truth is from God's perspective and He, undoubtedly, doesn't have the same problem with some of your husband's actions as you do. Our goal must not be to get our husbands to do what *we* want, but rather to release them to God so He can get them to do what *He* wants.

Distinguish carefully between what is truly right and wrong. If it doesn't fall clearly into either of those categories, keep your personal opinions to yourself. Or pray about them and then, as the Lord leads, reveal them for calm discussion. The Bible says, "Do not be rash with your mouth, and let not your heart utter anything hastily before God. For God is in heaven, and you on earth; therefore let your words be few" (Ecclesiastes 5:2). There are times when we are just to listen and not offer advice, to support and not offer constructive criticism.

I'm not for a moment suggesting that you become a timid doormat who doesn't ever confront your husband with the truth—especially when it's for his greater good. By all means you must clearly communicate your thoughts and feelings. But once he has heard them, don't continue to press him until it becomes a point of contention and strife.

If you *do* have to say words that are hard to hear, ask God to help you discern when your husband would be most open to hearing them. Pray for the right words and for his heart to be totally receptive. I know that's difficult to do if you have a few choice words you're dying to let loose. But hard as it may seem, it's best to let God hear them first so He can temper them with His Spirit. This is especially true when talking has ceased altogether and every word only brings more pain. I wish I had learned earlier to pray before I spoke. My words too often set up a defensive reaction in my husband that produced harsh words we both regret. He received my suggestions as pressure to do or be something, even though I always had his best interests at heart. It had to come to him from God.

When we live by the power of God rather than our flesh, we don't have to strive for power with our words. "For the kingdom of God is not in word but in power" (1 Corinthians 4:20). It's not the words we speak that make a difference, it is the power of God accompanying them. You'll be amazed at how much power your words have when you pray before you speak them. You'll be even more amazed at what can happen when you shut up and let God work.

Believer or Not

If your husband is not a believer, you probably already know how much good it does to keep talking to him about the Lord if he didn't respond the first number of times. It's not that you can't ever say anything to him, but if what you say is always met with indifference or irritation, the next step is to keep silent and pray. The Bible says a wife can win over her husband without saying anything, because what he *observes* in his wife speaks more loudly than what she tells him. "They, without a word, may be won by the conduct of their wives" (1 Peter 3:1,2).

God says He speaks of things that are not as though they were. You can do that, too. You can say, "I'm not going to pretend, but I'm going to speak of things that are *not* part of my husband's life as though they *were* a part of it. Even though he doesn't have faith, I'm going to pray for him as if he does." Of course you can't force him to do something he doesn't want to do, but you can access God's power through praying for His voice to penetrate your husband's soul. No matter how long you have to pray for your husband to come to know the Lord, even if it takes his whole life, the time will not be wasted. In the meantime, whether your husband is a believer or not, you can still pray all the prayers in this book for him and expect to see significant answers to them.

Creating a Home

I don't care how liberated you are, when you are married there will always be two areas that will ultimately be your responsibility: home and children. Even if you are the only one working and your husband stays home to keep the house and tend the kids, you will still be expected to see that the heart of your home is a peaceful sanctuary—a source of contentment, acceptance, rejuvenation, nurturing, rest, and love for your family. On top of this, you will also be expected to be sexually appealing, a good cook, a great mother, and physically, emotionally, and spiritually fit. It's overwhelming to most women, but the good news is that you don't have to do it all on your own. You can seek God's help.

Ask the Lord to show you how to make your home a safe haven that builds up your family—a place where creativity flows and communication is ongoing. Ask God to help you keep the house clean, the laundry done, the kitchen in order, the pantry and the refrigerator full, and the beds made. These are basic things a man may not compliment his wife on every day (or ever), but he will notice if they are *not* done. My husband may not look in the cupboard for a light bulb or a battery for months. But when he does, he wants it to be there. Nor does he want to come home late from work one night and find that there is no bread for a sandwich. I do my best to make sure it is there. I ask God to help me maintain a house that my husband is pleased to come home to and bring his friends. It's not necessary to have expensive furniture or a decorator in order to do all that. My first home was small and had second-hand furniture I bought from yard sales. I painted the entire place myself (with the help of a girlfriend) and made it look attractive. It just takes some thought and a little care.

Part of making a house a home is allowing your husband to be the head so you can be the heart. Trying to be both is too much. God placed the husband as the head over the family, whether he deserves it or not and whether he rises up to take his position or not. It's God's order of things. This doesn't mean that one position is more important than the other. They work together. If your husband is to be the head of the house, you must allow him that headship. If you are to be the heart of the home, you still must take the steps necessary to do so, even if you are a major contributor to the financial support. Trying to reverse that keeps a constant struggle going.

This doesn't mean that the wife can't work and the husband can't care for the home; it's the attitudes of the heart and head that makes the difference. There were weeks of time during the finishing of each book I've written when my husband took care of the house and the children so I could meet the deadline. It never minimized his headship or caused me to usurp his position. It was something he did for me. There were times he needed me to work so he could rest. It's what I did for him. It's a delicate balance for most people, so it's best to pray that the integrity of the two positions in the home—head and heart—are not compromised.

Keeping order in the home doesn't mean it has to be perfect, but it shouldn't be out of control. If you are working as hard as he is to bring home a paycheck, the responsibilities should be shared in the home. If he doesn't want to share them, spending a certain amount of money for someone to help you a few hours a week is a lot cheaper than a divorce, a chiropractor, a therapist, a medical doctor, or a funeral. Ask God to show you about that.

Everything I've said about the home goes for your body, soul, and spirit as well. Some effort must be put into maintaining them. I once heard a radio talk show where a woman called in to complain to a popular psychologist that her husband told her he no longer found her attractive. The host said, "What are you doing to make yourself attractive?" The caller had no answer. The point is, being attractive doesn't just happen. Even the most gorgeous women in the world do much to maintain their attractiveness. Queen Esther was one of the most beautiful women in her country and she still spent a year beautifying herself before she met the king.

We have to ask ourselves the same question. "What am I doing to make myself attractive to my husband?" Do I keep myself clean and smelling good? Do I see that my internal self is cleansed and rejuvenated with regular exercise? Do I preserve my strength and vitality with a healthful diet? Do I dress attractively? And most important: Do I spend time alone with God every day? I guarantee that the more time you spend with the Lord, the more radiant you will become. "Charm is deceitful and beauty is passing, but a woman who fears the LORD, she shall be praised" (Proverbs 31:30).

You can't afford not to make this investment in yourself, your health, and your future. It's not selfish to do it. It's selfish *not* to do it. Pray for God to show you what steps to take and then enable you to take them. Invite the Holy Spirit to dwell in you *and* your home.

Letting Go of Expectations

Shortly after we were married, my husband called from work and said he wanted me to prepare a certain chicken dish for dinner. I went to the store, got the food, prepared the dish, and when he came home, he walked in the door and said bluntly, "I don't feel like chicken tonight, I want lamb chops." I needn't tell you the thoughts that went through my mind because I'm sure you already know them. This was not an isolated incident. Similar ones happened far too frequently. I can't count the number of times Michael promised to be home for dinner and called ten minutes *after* dinner was ready to say he was going to work late and would eat out with his coworkers. I finally learned that it did no good to be angry, hurt, or resentful. That only made matters worse. It made him defensive because he thought I didn't understand his situation. I realized it was healthier for both of us if I rearranged my expectations. From then on, I prepared meals as if only I and the children would be eating them. If Michael was able to join us, it was a pleasant surprise. If he didn't, I could live with it.

I've learned that when disappointing things happen, it's best to remind myself of my husband's good qualities. I recount how he sometimes helps with the household chores and the cooking. He is faithful and does not give me reason to doubt it. He is a believer who goes to church, reads his Bible, prays, and has high moral standards. He loves me and our children. He uses his talents for God's glory. He is a good and generous provider. Things could be a lot worse, so I won't complain about whether he's home for dinner or not.

I think if I could help a new wife in any area, it would be to discourage her from coming into her marriage with a big list of expectations and then being upset when her husband doesn't live up to them. Of course there are some basics that should be agreed upon before the wedding date, such as fidelity, financial support, honesty, kindness, basic decency, high moral standards, physical and emotional love, and protection. When you don't get those things, you can ask for them. When you still don't get them, you can pray.

But when it comes to specifics, you can't require one person to meet all of your needs. The pressure to do that and fulfill your dreams at the same time can be overwhelming to a man. Instead, take your needs to God in prayer and look to *Him* for the answers. If we try to control our husbands by having a big list for them to live up to and then are angry and disappointed when they can't, *we* are the ones in error. The biggest problems in my marriage occurred when my expectations of what I thought Michael should be or do didn't coincide with the reality of who he was.

Let go of as many expectations as possible. The changes you try to make happen in your husband, or that your husband tries to make in himself to please you, are doomed to failure and will bring disappointment for you both. Instead, ask God to make any necessary changes. He will do a far better job because "whatever God does, it shall be forever. Nothing can be added to it, and nothing taken from it" (Ecclesiastes 3:14). Accept your husband the way he is and pray for him to grow. Then when change happens, it will be because God has worked it in him and it will be lasting. "My soul, wait silently for God alone, for my expectation is from Him" (Psalm 62:5). Your greatest expectations must be from God, not your husband.

With All Due Respect

It's interesting that God requires the husband to *love* his wife, but the wife is required to have *respect* for her husband. "Let each one of you in particular so love his own wife as himself, and let the wife see that she respects her husband" (Ephesians 5:33). I assume no woman would marry a man she didn't love, but too often a wife loses respect for her husband after they've been married awhile. Loss of respect seems to precede loss of love and is more hurtful to a man than we realize.

The consequences of losing respect for your husband can be very serious. King David's wife, Michal, watched her husband dancing for joy before the Lord in front of the people, without his kingly clothing and in his undergarments, as the ark of the covenant was being brought into the city. Michal not only didn't share his joy, she had contempt for him (2 Samuel 6:16). She was critical instead of trying to understand the situation from God's perspective. She paid a dear price for her lack of respect; God's judgment caused her to be unable to ever bear children. I believe we not only bring defeat into our marriages and our husbands when we don't have respect for them, but it shuts the door to new life in us as well.

In another example, Queen Vashti refused to go to the king at his command. The king was giving a feast for his friends, he was in a party mood, and he wanted to show off his beautiful wife. All he asked of her was that she put on her royal clothes, don her royal crown, and make a royal appearance to the people he was entertaining. She declined, knowing full well it would be humiliating for him. "Queen Vashti refused to come at the king's command brought by his eunuchs; therefore the king was furious, and his anger burned within him" (Esther 1:12). The result was that Vashti lost her position as queen. She not only wronged her husband, the king, but the people as well. Unless a wife wants to lose her position as queen of her husband's heart, and hurt her family and friends besides, she mustn't humiliate her husband no matter how much she thinks he deserves it. The price is too high.

If this has already happened to you, and you know you've shown disrespect for your husband, confess it to God right now. Say, "Lord, I confess I do not esteem my husband the way Your Word says to. There is a wall in my heart that I know was erected as a protection against being hurt. But I am ready to let it come down so that my heart can heal. I confess the times I have shown a lack of respect for him. I confess my disrespectful attitude and words as sin against You. Show me how to dismantle this barrier over my emotions that keeps me from having the unconditional love You want me to have. Tear down the wall of hardness around my heart and show me how to respect my husband the way You want me to. Give me *Your* heart for him, Lord, and help me to see him the way You see him."

Praying like this will free you to see your man's potential for greatness, as opposed to his flaws. It will enable you to say something positive that will encourage, build up, give life, and make the marriage better. Love is diminished if we dwell on the negatives. Love grows if we focus on the positive. When you have God's heart for your husband, you will be able to see through new eyes. There are times when you can't understand where your husband is coming from, what he is feeling, and why he is doing the things he does, unless you have the discernment of God. Ask God to give it to you.

When you are praying for yourself—his wife—remember this model of a good wife from the Bible. It says she takes care of her home and runs it well. She knows how to buy and sell and make wise investments. She keeps herself healthy and strong and dresses attractively. She works diligently and has skills which are marketable. She is giving and conscientiously prepares for the future. She contributes to her husband's good reputation. She is strong, solid, honorable, and not afraid of growing older. She speaks wisely and kindly. She doesn't sit around doing nothing, but carefully watches what goes on in her home. Her children and her husband praise her. She doesn't rely on charm and beauty but knows that the fear of the Lord is what is most attractive. She supports her husband and still has a fruitful life of her own which speaks loudly for itself (Proverbs 31).

This is an amazing woman, the kind of woman we can become only through God's enablement and our own surrendering. The bottom line is that she is a woman whose husband trusts her because "she does him good and not evil all the days of her life." I believe the most important "good" a wife can do for her husband is pray. Shall we?

Prayer

Lord, Help me to be a good wife. I fully realize that I don't have what it takes to be one without Your help. Take my selfishness, impatience, and irritability and turn them into kindness, long-suffering, and the willingness to bear all things. Take my old emotional habits, mindsets, automatic reactions, rude assumptions, and self-protective stance, and make me patient, kind, good, faithful, gentle, and self-controlled. Take the hardness of my heart and break down the walls with Your battering ram of revelation. Give me a new heart and work in me Your love, peace, and joy (Galatians 5:22,23). I am not able to rise above who I am at this moment. Only You can transform me.

Show me where there is sin in my heart, especially with regard to my husband. I confess the times I've been unloving, critical, angry, resentful, disrespectful, or unforgiving toward him. Help me to put aside any hurt, anger, or disappointment I feel and forgive him the way You do—totally and completely, no looking back. Make me a tool of reconciliation, peace, and healing in this marriage. Enable us to communicate well and rescue us from the threshold of separation where the realities of divorce begin.

Make me my husband's helpmate, companion, champion, friend, and support. Help me to create a peaceful, restful, safe place for him to come home to. Teach me how to take care of myself and stay attractive to him. Grow me into a creative and confident woman who is rich in mind, soul, and spirit. Make me the kind of woman he can be proud to say is his wife.

I lay all my expectations at Your cross. I release my husband from the burden of fulfilling me in areas where I should be looking to You. Help me to accept him the way he is and not try to change him. I realize that in some ways he may never change, but at the same time, I release him to change in ways I never thought he could. I leave any changing that needs to be done in Your hands, fully accepting that neither of us is perfect and never will be. Only You, Lord, are perfect and I look to You to perfect us.

Teach me how to pray for my husband and make my prayers a true language of love. Where love has died, create new love between us. Show me what unconditional love really is and how to communicate it in a way he can clearly perceive. Bring unity between us so that we can be in agreement about everything (Amos 3:3). May the God of patience and comfort grant us to be like-minded toward one another, according to Christ Jesus (Romans 15:5). Make us a team, not pursuing separate, competitive, or independent lives, but working together, overlooking each other's faults and weaknesses for the greater good of the marriage. Help us to pursue the things which make for peace and the things by which one may edify another (Romans 14:19). May we be "perfectly joined together in the same mind and in the same judgment" (1 Corinthians 1:10).

I pray that our commitment to You and to one another will grow stronger and more passionate every day. Enable him to be the head of the home as You made him to be, and show me how to support and respect him as he rises to that place of leadership. Help me to understand his dreams and see things from his perspective. Reveal to me what he wants and needs and show me potential problems before they arise. Breathe Your life into this marriage.

Make me a new person, Lord. Give me a fresh perspective, a positive outlook, and a renewed relationship with the man You've given me. Help me see him with new eyes, new appreciation, new love, new compassion, and new acceptance. Give my husband a new wife, and let it be me.

POWER TOOLS

Whatever things you ask when you pray, believe
that you receive them, and you will have them. And
whenever you stand praying, if you have anything
against anyone, forgive him, that your Father in
heaven may also forgive you your trespasses.
MARK 11:24,25

Be kind to one another, tenderhearted, forgiving
one another, even as God in Christ forgave you.
EPHESIANS 4:32

Ask, and it will be given to you; seek, and you will
find; knock, and it will be opened to you. For
everyone who asks receives, and he who seeks finds,
and to him who knocks it will be opened.
MATTHEW 7:7,8

Through wisdom a house is built, and by
understanding it is established; by knowledge
the rooms are filled with all precious
and pleasant riches.
PROVERBS 24:3,4

Let us not grow weary while doing good, for in due
season we shall reap if we do not lose heart.
GALATIANS 6:9

CHAPTER TWO

His Work

Bill seldom works. He's willing to let his wife, Kim, support the family while he pursues his dream. The problem is that Kim is not content to bear the entire burden of supporting the family on her shoulders indefinitely, and Bill has been pursuing his dream for seventeen years with nothing to show for it. I believe the root of Bill's inactivity is fear. He's afraid that if he doesn't get the job of his dreams, he will end up in a job he hates and be stuck there forever.

Steven is working himself to death. He can never rest and enjoy the success of his labor. He seldom spends time with his family, and his teenagers are fast approaching adulthood. He doesn't work that hard because he has to, but because he is afraid. He fears that if he ever stops, he will be worth nothing in everyone's eyes, including his own.

These are extreme examples of how a man can relate to his work. On one hand is laziness—avoiding work out of selfishness, fear, lack of confidence, depression, or apprehension about the future. Of the lazy, God says, "As a door turns on its hinges, so does the lazy man on his bed" (Proverbs 26:14). "Drowsiness will clothe a man with rags" (Proverbs 23:21). "The way of the lazy man is like a hedge of thorns" (Proverbs 15:19). "The desire of the lazy man kills him, for his hands refuse to labor" (Proverbs 21:25). In other words, a lazy man will never get anywhere, he will never have anything, he will have a rough road ahead, and it will ultimately destroy him.

The opposite extreme is workaholism—obsessing over work to the exclusion of all else and losing one's life in the process. Of the workaholic, God says, "So are the ways of everyone who is greedy for gain; it takes away the life of its owners" (Proverbs 1:19). "I looked on all the works that my hands had done and on the labor in which I had toiled; and indeed all was vanity and grasping for the wind. There was no profit under the sun" (Ecclesiastes 2:11). In other words, workaholism is draining and pointless.

Neither extreme promotes happiness and fulfillment. Only a perfect balance between the two, which God can help a man find, will ever bring that quality of life.

What causes a man to go to either extreme can be, oddly enough, the same reason: fear. That's because a man's identity is often very tied up in his work. He needs to be appreciated and he needs to win, and his work is often a means of seeing both happen. It frightens him to think he may never experience either. If he is doing work that is demeaning to him, he feels devalued as a person. If his work is not successful, he feels like a loser.

God recognizes that a man's work is a source of fulfillment to him. He says there is nothing better than for a man to "enjoy the good of all his labor—it is the gift of God"

(Ecclesiastes 3:13). The fact that many men are not fulfilled in their work has less to do with what their work is than with whether or not they have a sense of purpose. A man who doesn't have that can eventually come to a place where he has worked hard and long for so little reward that he no longer sees a future for himself—at least not one worth living. If there's also the specter of age creeping up on him, he may hear words in his head like, "You're not valuable to anyone." "You're replaceable." "You can't do what you used to." "You're too old to learn new things." "You don't have it." "You have no purpose." This is a dangerous place for a man to be.

Gary, his father, and his grandfather all had difficulty making a living. In fact, it was very late in each of their lives before they were even able to discern what they were supposed to be doing. They went from job to job without any clear leading. They struggled financially. None of them had parents who prayed for them to have their gifts and talents revealed, to know the calling of God on their lives, to have doors opened to them, and to become all they were created to be. History tends to repeat itself without the intervention of God.

I've observed that people who have had actively praying parents seem to find their life's work early. Their careers may not take off immediately, but they have a sense of purpose and destiny that propels them in the right direction. They don't live with the frustration and aimlessness that the others do. While many parents have an agenda for their children, not enough of them seek out *God's* plan for their lives. When a child's life is left to chance that way, a kind of vocational wandering can result. There is needless floundering, disappointment, doubt, and despair as he tries to carve out a place for himself. If your husband had that kind of start, your prayers can change his life.

If your husband didn't have praying parents, you can step in the gap. You can pray for his eyes to be opened to see what God wants him to do, and where God is leading. Your prayers can help him feel appreciated and encouraged enough to recognize he has worth no matter what he does. You can assure him that God has uniquely gifted him with ability and talent and has something good ahead for him. Then pray for God to reveal it and open a door of opportunity which no man can shut. Your prayers can pave a path for him.

Even if your husband already has a successful career, it's still good to pray that he is where God wants him to be and that everything will continue to go smoothly. My husband, who is a songwriter and record producer, said he felt my prayers have prevented him from working with the wrong clients. He has never worked with anyone who is difficult, weird, evil, or unsuitable, which is nothing less than a miracle in his business. He knew I always prayed that God would lead him to the right people and remove from his path those who would be trouble. While our prayers cannot ensure a trouble-free road for our husbands, they can certainly steer them clear of many problems.

If your husband is a hard worker, make sure he has times of rest and enjoyment—to do things that entertain him and give him a reprieve from the weight of a lifetime of supporting a family. Men need periods of refreshing. If they don't have them, they are prone to burnout and temptation of all kinds. Your prayers can help your husband understand that the true meaning of life doesn't come from work, it comes from following God. Let's pray for our husbands to find that perfect balance.

Prayer

Lord, I pray that You would bless the work of my husband's hands. May his labor bring not only favor, success, and prosperity, but great fulfillment as well. If the work he is doing is not in line with Your perfect will for his life, reveal it to him. Show him what he should do differently and guide him down the right path. Give him strength, faith, and a vision for the future so he can rise above any propensity for laziness. May he never run from work out of fear, selfishness, or a desire to avoid responsibility. On the other hand, help him to see that he doesn't have to work himself to death for man's approval, or grasp for gain beyond what is a gift from You. Give him the ability to enjoy his success without striving for more. Help him to excel, but free him from the pressure to do so.

I pray that You will be Lord over his work, and may he bring You into every aspect of it. Give him enough confidence in the gifts You've placed in him to be able to seek, find, and do good work. Open up doors of opportunity for him that no man can close. Develop his skills so that they grow more valuable with each passing year. Show me what I can do to encourage him.

I pray that his work will be established, secure, successful, satisfying, and financially rewarding. May he not be "lagging in diligence, [but] fervent in spirit, serving the Lord" (Romans 12:11). Let him be like a tree planted by the stream of Your living water, which brings forth fruit in due season. May he never wither under pressure, but grow strong and prosper (Psalm 1:3).

POWER TOOLS

Do you see a man who excels in his work?
He will stand before kings; he will not stand
before unknown men.
PROVERBS 22:29

Do not overwork to be rich; because of your own understanding, cease! Will you set your eyes on that
which is not? For riches certainly make themselves
wings; they fly away like an eagle toward heaven.
PROVERBS 23:4,5

For what profit is it to a man if he gains the whole
world, and loses his own soul? Or what will a man
give in exchange for his soul?
MATTHEW 16:26

Because of laziness the building decays, and through
idleness of hands the house leaks.
ECCLESIASTES 10:18

Let the beauty of the LORD our God be upon us, and
establish the work of our hands for us; yes, establish
the work of our hands.
PSALM 90:17

CHAPTER THREE

His Finances

*M*uch of who your husband is and what he experiences in life is wrapped up in how he relates to his finances. Is he giving or miserly? Is he thankful or envious of others? Is money a blessing or a curse? Is he wise or reckless with what he has? Is he in agreement with you as to how it is to be spent, or does your marriage exhibit financial strife? Nothing puts more pressure on a marriage than financial irresponsibility, lack of money, and huge debt. Only when we recognize that all we have comes from God and seek to make Him Lord over it can we avoid the pitfalls that money, or the lack of it, brings.

Although my husband has always made a good living, the nature of his business is "feast or famine" with regard to when and how much money comes in. One year there was a recession in the music business and everybody felt it. Even the companies who owed us money withheld payment because of their own lack of cash flow. It was a frightening time, but it would have been much worse if we hadn't had faith in the Lord and committed our finances to Him. Our comfort came in knowing that we had obeyed God in tithing our money to the church. "Bring all the tithes into the storehouse" and see if He "will not open for you the windows of heaven and pour out for you such blessing that there will not be room enough to receive it" (Malachi 3:10). We had also been faithful to give to the poor and those in need. "Blessed is he who considers the poor; the LORD will deliver him in time of trouble. The LORD will preserve him and keep him alive, and he will be blessed on the earth" (Psalm 41:1,2). We also knew the Bible promises that "those who seek the LORD shall not lack any good thing" (Psalm 34:10). We certainly were seeking the Lord. We believed that by looking to God as our source and living in obedience to His ways, He would provide for us and we would have everything we need. He did and we do.

So many money problems can be solved by putting all finances under God's covering and doing what He says to do with them. That means giving when He says to give. When you do, God promises to deliver you, protect you, bless you, heal you, and keep you alive. When you don't, you will experience the same desolation the poor do. "Whoever shuts his ears to the cry of the poor will also cry himself and not be heard" (Proverbs 21:13). Not giving cuts off your own ability to enjoy what you have and leads to lifelong difficulties.

To be sure, there are wealthy people who do not give. But if you were to check closely into their lives, you'd find that they are missing many of the Lord's blessings. The blessings of wholeness, protection, love, peace, health, and fulfillment continually elude them and they don't know why. They gain wealth but lose the ability to enjoy it, all because they don't know that the key to life is knowing the Lord and living His way. This means giving time, energy, love, talent, and finances according to His direction.

Pray that your husband gets hold of this key to life and understands God's will for his finances. Pray that he becomes a giving person who is content to live within his means and not always strive for more. I'm not saying he should never try to increase his earnings—quite the contrary. A man deserves to earn what his work is worth and his wife should pray he does. Backbreaking drudgery that leads to gut-wrenching poverty and with it bitterness, anguish, sickness, and envy should not be accepted as a way of life. By all means pray that the storehouses of blessing will be opened upon him, but pray that it all comes from the hand of God. "The blessing of the LORD makes one rich, and He adds no sorrow with it" (Proverbs 10:22).

It may not be possible to use prayer to avoid every financial problem because God sometimes uses finances to get our attention and teach us things. But your prayers will certainly help protect your husband from unnecessary struggle and loss. God's desire is to bless those who have obedient, grateful, and giving hearts, whose true treasure is in the Lord. "Where your treasure is, there your heart will be also" (Matthew 6:21). God wants your husband to find his treasure in Him, not in his finances.

Prayer

Lord, I commit our finances to You. Be in charge of them and use them for Your purposes. May we both be good stewards of all that You give us, and walk in total agreement as to how it is to be dispersed. I pray that we will learn to live free of burdensome debt. Where we have not been wise, bring restoration and give us guidance. Show me how I can help increase our finances and not decrease them unwisely. Help us to remember that all we have belongs to You, and to be grateful for it.

I pray that (husband's name) will find it easy to give to You and to others as You have instructed in Your Word. Give him wisdom to handle money wisely. Help him make good decisions as to how he spends. Show him how to plan for the future. I pray that he will find the perfect balance between spending needlessly and being miserly. May he always be paid well for the work he does, and may his money not be stolen, lost, devoured, destroyed, or wasted. Multiply it so that what he makes will go a long way. I pray that he will not be anxious about finances, but will seek Your kingdom first, knowing that as he does, we will have all we need (Luke 12:31).

POWER TOOLS

Do not seek what you should eat or what you
should drink, nor have an anxious mind. For all
these things the nations of the world seek after,
and your Father knows that you need these things.
But seek the kingdom of God, and all these
things shall be added to you.
LUKE 12:29-31

As for every man to whom God has given riches and
wealth, and given him power to eat of it, to
receive his heritage and rejoice in his labor;
this is the gift of God.
ECCLESIASTES 5:19

He who gives to the poor will not lack, but he
who hides his eyes will have many curses.
PROVERBS 28:27

I have been young, and now am old; yet I have not
seen the righteous forsaken, nor his descendants
begging bread.
PSALM 37:25

My God shall supply all your need according to
His riches in glory by Christ Jesus.
PHILIPPIANS 4:19

CHAPTER FOUR

His Sexuality

*W*e're hitting the top priorities in a man's life right away in this book. I feel if we can contribute to our husbands' happiness in these areas most dear to their hearts, we will have greater success making inroads in other areas that are crucial to their well-being.

After twenty years of praying with women about their failing, struggling, unfulfilling, or dead marriages, I've observed that frequently the sexual relationship is a low priority in their minds. It isn't that the wife cares nothing about that part of her life. It's that there are so many other things screaming for her attention, such as raising children, work, finances, managing a home, emotional stress, exhaustion, sickness, and marital strife. In the wife's juggling of priorities, sex can end up on the bottom of her list. Some women allow week after week, month after month, six months, a year, or even more to go by without having sexual relations with their husbands for one reason or another. When disaster hits, they are surprised. Even though the wife may have felt fine about this arrangement, her husband was being neglected in an important part of his being.

For a wife, sex comes out of affection. She doesn't want to be affectionate with a man who makes her feel angry, hurt, lonely, disappointed, overworked, unsupported, un-cared for, or abandoned. But for a husband, sex is pure need. His eyes, ears, brain, and emotions get clouded if he doesn't have that release. He has trouble hearing anything his wife says or seeing what she needs when that area of his being is neglected. Wives sometimes have it backwards. They think, *We can have sex after we get these other issues settled.* But actually there is a far greater chance of settling the other issues if sex comes first.

That's why it's important to make sex a matter of pri-ority in your marriage. Whether all conditions are perfect or whether you feel like it or not isn't the point. The point is meeting the needs of your husband and keeping communi-cation lines open. A man can easily be made to feel in-significant, beaten down, discouraged, destroyed, or tempted in this area of his being. There is probably no more important means of fulfillment for a man, and no area where he is more vulnerable.

Sexual problems are quite common because many women don't have a clear grasp of what God's view is on the subject. But the Bible is crystal clear. "The wife does not have authority over her own body but the husband does. And likewise the husband does not have authority over his own body but the wife does. Do not deprive one another ex-cept with consent for a time, that you may give yourselves to fasting and prayer; and come together again so that Satan does not tempt you because of your lack of self-control" (1 Corinthians 7:4,5). Sex between a husband and wife is God's idea. Unless we're fasting and praying for weeks at a time, or are experiencing physical infirmity or separation, there is no excuse not to engage in it regularly.

When we're married, our bodies are not our own. We *owe* each other physical attention and we're not to deprive one another. The frequency of sex depends on the *other person's* need, not ours alone. If your attitude about having sex comes down to only what *you* need or what *you* don't want, then you don't have God's perspective. He says our body is to be used to comfort and complete the *other* person. Something is built up in the man and the marriage when this need is met by his wife. Something is diminished when it is not. You leave yourselves open for temptation, and far more destruction than you can imagine, when this area of intimate communication is neglected. It can happen to anyone, and that's why the sexual aspect of your marriage and your husband's sexuality need to be covered in prayer. And it's best to start praying about it *before* you have to.

If your husband desires sex more frequently and you are the one keeping it from happening, pray for God to help you change your ways. I've found that the most difficult time to deal with the issue of sex is when the children are small and can't do much for themselves. By the time you get them in bed, you are exhausted and ready to drop. You're thinking about getting to sleep as soon as possible, while your husband has been making other plans for you. Your options are to totally shut him down and say, "Forget about it. I'm tired," or communicate how exhausted you are and hope *he'll* say, "No problem. You get some rest," or proceed with a bad attitude and make him feel guilty or angry. But I've found a fourth option which works much better. Try this and see if it doesn't work for you.

When your husband communicates to you what he has in mind, as only a husband can do, don't roll your eyes and sigh deeply. Instead, say, "Okay, give me fifteen minutes." (Or ten or twenty, or whatever you need.) During that time, do something to make yourself feel attractive. For example, take a shower or a relaxing bath. Put on scented body lotion or his favorite perfume. (Have perfume you wear only for these times alone with him.) Comb your hair. Wash your face and prepare it with products that make your skin look dewy and fresh. Put on lip gloss and blush. Slip into lingerie you know he finds irresistible. Don't worry about your imperfections; he's not thinking about them. If you feel self-conscious, wear a beautiful nightgown that covers areas that bother you. While you're doing this, pray for God to give you renewed energy, strength, vitality, and a good attitude. Hopefully, when you're ready, your husband will find you were worth the wait. You'll be surprised at how much better a sex partner you are when you feel good about yourself. He'll be happier and you'll both sleep better. This is a small investment of time to see great rewards in your marriage.

Sometimes there is the opposite situation, where the wife is sexually neglected by her husband. His lack of interest can happen for many reasons—physical, mental, or emotional. But if he is content to go month after month without sex, then something is wrong. If there is no physical problem hindering him, maybe he's having deep feelings of failure, disappointment, depression, or hopelessness that need to be addressed. Prayer can help reveal what the problem is and how to solve it. Get professional help if you need to. It's cheaper than a divorce or the physical, emotional, and mental ravages of a dead marriage. Don't let negative emotions like resentment, bitterness, self-pity, and unforgiveness build up in you. Keep yourself healthy and attractive. If you don't think highly enough of yourself to take care of your body, do it as an act of kindness for *him*. Have special lingerie that *he* likes and put it on when you're with him. Get a new hairstyle. Surprise him with a new attitude. Keep your mind refreshed and growing. Basically, *don't do nothing*.

Bad things develop when the sexual part of a marriage is neglected. Don't let that happen to you. Keep an eye on the calendar and refuse to allow much time to go by without coming together physically. If it has been too long, ask God to show you why and help you remedy the situation. And remember, it's never too late to pray for sexual purity, no matter what has occurred in either of your pasts. Sometimes sexual problems in a marriage happen as a result of sexual experiences before the marriage. Pray to be set free and healed of those memories. Purity happens the moment it takes root in the heart. Prayer is where it starts. Don't jeopardize or forfeit what God has for your marriage by neglecting to pray for this vital area of your life.

Prayer

Lord, bless my husband's sexuality and make it an area of great fulfillment for him. Restore what needs to be restored, balance what needs to be balanced. Protect us from apathy, disappointment, criticism, busyness, unforgiveness, deadness, or disinterest. I pray that we make time for one another, communicate our true feelings openly, and remain sensitive to what each other needs.

Keep us sexually pure in mind and body, and close the door to anything lustful or illicit that seeks to encroach upon us. Deliver us from the bondage of past mistakes. Remove from our midst the effects of any sexual experience—in thought or deed—that happened outside of our relationship. Take away anyone or anything from our lives that would inspire temptation to infidelity. Help us to "abstain from sexual immorality" so that each of us will know "how to possess his own vessel in sanctification and honor" (1 Thessalonians 4:3-5). I pray that we will desire each other and no one else. Show me how to make myself attractive and desirable to him and be the kind of partner he needs. I pray that neither of us will ever be tempted to think about seeking fulfillment elsewhere.

I realize that an important part of my ministry to my husband is sexual. Help me to never use it as a weapon or a means of manipulation by giving and withholding it for selfish reasons. I commit this area of our lives to You, Lord. May it be continually new and alive. Make it all that You created it to be.

POWER TOOLS

Flee sexual immorality. Every sin that a man does is outside the body, but he who commits sexual immorality sins against his own body. Or do you not know that your body is the temple of the Holy Spirit who is in you, whom you have from God, and you are not your own? For you were bought at a price; therefore glorify God in your body and in your spirit, which are God's.

1 CORINTHIANS 6:18-20

The body is not for sexual immorality but for the
Lord, and the Lord for the body.
1 CORINTHIANS 6:13

Drink water from your own cistern, and running
water from your own well. Should your fountains be
dispersed abroad, streams of water in the streets? Let
them be only your own, and not for strangers with
you. Let your fountain be blessed, and rejoice with
the wife of your youth. As a loving deer and a
graceful doe, let her breasts satisfy you at all times;
and always be enraptured with her love.
PROVERBS 5:15-19

CHAPTER FIVE

His Affection

Tom and Patti had been married a number of years before she actually had a serious talk with him about his lack of affection. Tom was a wonderful husband in every other way and their sexual relationship was good, but apart from the sexual act there was no affection. It wasn't because Tom didn't love Patti—he adored her. It was because affection was something he grew up without as a child. Patti felt guilty about the way she was feeling and didn't want to criticize or hurt Tom, but she had not known affection as a child, either, and that's why she needed it so in her marriage. Each time Patti confronted Tom about this problem he would try to change, but soon things were back to the way they had been. This led to great frustration and hurt in both of them. Eventually Patti became hopeless and felt like she was dying inside. She didn't see how she could live the rest of her life without affection, but she saw no hope of Tom's ever being any different.

Finally, Patti's misery forced her to take the problem to her prayer partners. They diligently covered it in prayer every week and as they prayed, God worked on Patti. He spoke to her about obeying Him in the area of eating right and getting proper exercise—an area where she had always been in rebellion. When she totally submitted to God regarding this and started doing the things He had been telling her to do, she began to feel better about herself and realized that she *deserved* to be treated affectionately by her husband. She didn't have to feel guilty about wanting affection because the Lord wanted that for her, too. Soon she felt the leading of God to confront Tom about it again. This time it would be different because she was now led by the Holy Spirit, and she and her prayer partners had been praying for a miraculous transformation in Tom.

"It took courage for me to even speak of this again," she told me. "I was afraid it could lead to divorce because we were both so hurt and saw no hope in each other. But God gave me the ability to speak in love the words that needed to be said, and this time the conversation brought immediate breakthrough."

"The turning point came," Tom recalled, "when Patti said to me, 'Honey, how can someone as wonderful as you, with all your attributes, someone I love and trust so much, not be able to be affectionate?'"

"Because I said words that affirmed him," Patti explained further, "it gave him hope that it was worth trying again."

Tom proceeded differently this time. He took the problem to his own prayer group of men, who instantly rallied around him. They decided not only to support him daily in prayer, but also to keep him accountable to show some form of affection to Patti each day.

"This was something I welcomed, because I wanted to change," Tom said. "I love Patti and hated that I was hurting her. I wanted to be different and I knew that true transformation can only happen by the power of the Holy Spirit."

Every day for a number of weeks, one of the men from the group called Tom and said, "What have you done to show affection to Patti today?" They also suggested *ways* to show affection and affirm her. They told Tom to check in regularly with Patti and say, "How am I doing?" For someone whose heart had not been prepared by the Holy Spirit, this could have been extremely annoying. But because Tom welcomed the Lord's working in him, it brought no burden.

"Now the first thing he does when he comes home is give me a hug and a kiss," Patti said with a radiant smile. "I felt like a new person after five hugs."

Tom and Patti's situation is not a rare one. Many people, even godly men and women, live in marriages that are dead because there is no affection. And women endure it because their husbands are good in other ways, or they don't feel worthy enough to ask for affection. But this is not the way God designed the marital relationship. "Let the husband render to his wife the affection due her, and likewise also the wife to her husband" (1 Corinthians 7:3). There is "a time to embrace," the Bible says (Ecclesiastes 3:5). When you're married, it's definitely the time. Affection isn't at the top of a man's priority list because men often see sex and affection as being the same. A woman's greatest need is for affection. If you are in a marriage that lacks it, pray for the Holy Spirit's transformation.

Prayer

Lord, I pray for open physical affection between my husband and me. Enable each of us to lay aside self-consciousness or apathy and be effusive in our display of love. Help us to demonstrate how much we care for and value each other. Remind us throughout each day to affectionately touch one another in some way. Help us to not be cold, undemonstrative, uninterested, or remote. Enable us to be warm, tender, compassionate, loving, and adoring. Break through any hardheadedness on our part that refuses to change and grow. If one of us is less affectionate to the other's detriment, bring us into balance.

Where any lack of affection has planted a negative view of marriage in our children, or taught them an incorrect way of relating to a marriage partner, help us to model the right way so that they can observe it. Show us how to openly confess our errors to them and demonstrate our commitment to live differently.

Change our habits of indifference or busyness. May we not so take each other for granted that we don't make the effort to reach out and touch one another with affection. Help us not to weaken the marriage through neglect of this vital means of communication. I pray that we always "greet one another with a kiss of love" (1 Peter 5:14). I know that only the transforming power of the Holy Spirit can make changes that last. I trust You to transform us and make us the husband and wife You called us to be.

POWER TOOLS

If there is any consolation in Christ, if any comfort of love, if any fellowship of the Spirit, if any affection and mercy, fulfill my joy by being like-minded, having the same love, being of one accord, of one mind.
PHILIPPIANS 2:1,2

So husbands ought to love their own wives as their own bodies; he who loves his wife loves himself. For no one ever hated his own flesh, but nourishes and cherishes it, just as the Lord does the church.
EPHESIANS 5:28,29

Let each of you look out not only for his own interests, but also for the interests of others.
PHILIPPIANS 2:4

His left hand is under my head, and his right hand embraces me.
SONG OF SOLOMON 2:6

Let no one seek his own, but each one the other's well-being.
1 CORINTHIANS 10:24

CHAPTER SIX

His Temptations

From the time Michael and I were married, I prayed for God to remove temptation from our lives. I don't know if it has been the result of prayer or the fact that we both guard ourselves against such things, but we've never given each other a single moment of concern. I'm sure it's due more to the hand of God than the strength of human restraint, but both are important.

I know several couples who experienced adultery in their marriages, but because in each case there was a wife who was willing to pray and a husband open to allowing God to change and restore him, the marriages are still intact and successful today. Only prayer, a submitted heart, and the transforming power of the Holy Spirit can work those kinds of miracles.

I have another friend whose husband had numerous affairs before they finally divorced. Each time it was with one of her best friends. I questioned her choice of "friends," but I never questioned her godliness or commitment to pray. She prayed. But a heart that refuses to listen to the promptings of the Holy Spirit will not change, no matter how hard you pray.

Temptation is everywhere today and we're fools if we think we or our husbands can't be lured by it in some form or another. The Bible says, "The eyes of man are never satisfied" (Proverbs 27:20). If that's true, temptation is always a possibility and we must be ever watchful. Certain people are tempted by alcohol and drugs; others have a lust for money and power. Still others find food addictions, pornography, or sexual immorality to be irresistible lures. The enemy of our souls knows where our flesh is the weakest and he will put temptations in our paths at our most vulnerable points. The question is not whether there will be temptations, it's how we will handle them when they arise. I recommend praying through them. While prayer may not be able to stop a man from doing something he is determined to do, it *can* diminish the voices of temptation and strengthen his resolve. It can pave the way for him to make right choices.

The Bible says that God does not tempt us. It is our *desires* that draw us away to what entices us. It is our *desires* that cause us to sin and bring death into our lives. But "blessed is the man who endures temptation; for when he has been approved, he will receive the crown of life which the Lord has promised to those who love Him" (James 1:12). God wants us to get through temptation because He wants to bless us. But He needs to see if we can be trusted to chose His ways over our fleshly desires. He'll always give us a way out if we want it badly enough to seek Him for it.

The best time to start praying about this is *before* anything happens. Jesus instructed His disciples to "pray that you may not enter into temptation" (Luke 22:40). He said to be watchful because "the spirit indeed is willing, but the flesh is weak" (Mark 14:38). If your husband struggles in a certain area, pray that he will want to have godly prayer partners with whom he can share openly, be accountable, and receive prayer. Open confession before God and other believers does more to minimize the power of the tempter than anything else. Unfortunately, many men are reticent to reveal what tempts them most and so they shut off to the very thing that could protect them.

If after all your praying, your husband still falls into the hands of temptation, do not blame yourself. The decision is ultimately his. He has chosen to walk in the flesh and not in the Spirit. "Walk in the Spirit, and you shall not fulfill the lust of the flesh. For the flesh lusts against the Spirit, and the Spirit against the flesh; and these are contrary to one another, so that you do not do the things that you wish" (Galatians 5:16,17). Don't stop praying for him. No matter how hopeless it seems when you see him being tempted again and again, know that God has provided a means of escape and you may be the instrument He will use to help him find it. If there is no temptation problem in your marriage, be thankful and pray that it stays that way.

Prayer

Lord, I pray that You would strengthen my husband to resist any temptation that comes his way. Stamp it out of his mind before it ever reaches his heart or personal experience. Lead him not into temptation, but deliver him from evils such as adultery, pornography, drugs, alcohol, food addiction, gambling, and perversion. Remove temptation especially in the area of <u>(name specific temptation)</u>. Make him strong where he is weak. Help him to rise above anything that erects itself as a stronghold in his life. May he say, "I will set nothing wicked before my eyes; I hate the work of those who fall away; it shall not cling to me" (Psalm 101:3).

Lord, You've said that "Whoever has no rule over his own spirit is like a city broken down, without walls" (Proverbs 25:28). I pray that <u>(husband's name)</u> will not be broken down by the power of evil, but raised up by the power of God. Establish a wall of protection around him. Fill him with Your Spirit and flush out all that is not of You. Help him to take charge over his own spirit and have self-control to resist anything and anyone who becomes a lure. May he "abhor what is evil. Cling to what is good" (Romans 12:9). I pray that he will be repulsed by tempting situations. Give him courage to reject them. Teach him to walk in the Spirit so he will not fulfill the lust of the flesh.

POWER TOOLS

Let no one say when he is tempted, "I am
tempted by God"; for God cannot be tempted
by evil, nor does He Himself tempt anyone.
But each one is tempted when he is drawn
away by his own desires and enticed. Then,
when desire has conceived, it gives birth to
sin; and sin, when it is full-grown,
brings forth death.
JAMES 1:13-15

No temptation has overtaken you except such as is common to man; but God is faithful, who will not allow you to be tempted beyond what you are able, but with the temptation will also make the way of escape, that you may be able to bear it.
1 CORINTHIANS 10:13

Let us walk properly, as in the day, not in revelry and drunkenness, not in lewdness and lust, not in strife and envy. But put on the Lord Jesus Christ, and make no provision for the flesh, to fulfill its lusts.
ROMANS 13:13,14

Those who desire to be rich fall into temptation and a snare, and into many foolish and harmful lusts which drown men in destruction and perdition.
1 TIMOTHY 6:9

The works of the flesh are evident, which are: adultery, fornication, uncleanness, lewdness, idolatry, sorcery, hatred, contentions, jealousies, outbursts of wrath, selfish ambitions, dissensions, heresies, envy, murders, drunkenness, revelries, and the like; of which I tell you beforehand, just as I also told you in time past, that those who practice such things will not inherit the kingdom of God.
GALATIANS 5:19-21

CHAPTER SEVEN

His Mind

I used to attribute my husband's mind struggles to his musical genius. You know the artistic temperament—bright and brilliant on one hand, dark and moody on the other. When he would get down, the words in his mind told him he was going to fail, be worth nothing, that he was incapable of doing what he needed to do. It had no basis in reality because he had those kinds of thoughts even in the midst of his most productive and successful work. I didn't realize for a long time that the mind battles he endured did not have to be written off as "just the way he is." Nor did he have to fight them alone. If he and I were one, then an assault on his mind was an assault on me as well. I could stand with him in the battle by declaring, "This is not *God* speaking into my husband's life, it's the voice of the enemy. I'm not going to stand by and watch deadly games being played with his mind and our lives."

I decided to try my own experiment and "stand against the wiles of the devil" on his behalf (Ephesians 6:11). After all, the Bible talks about "praying always with all prayer and supplication in the Spirit, being watchful to this end with all perseverance and supplication for all the saints" (Ephesians 6:18). Surely "all the saints" is a category, even if it's not a description, which includes my husband. As I persevered in prayer for him over the next few months, I was amazed at the results. Not only did he become better able to control the thoughts in his mind, but eventually I could even see the onslaught coming and attack it in prayer before it gained a foothold. The more he saw my prayers answered, the more he realized where the lies were coming from and the less willing he was to believe them.

As I have traveled the country with my speaking engagements and talked with women from all walks of life, I have been amazed to see how universal this problem is. In fact, it didn't seem to matter what temperaments or backgrounds their husbands had, they experienced the same kind of lies in their mind. I finally realized that all men have an enemy who wants to undermine what God desires to do in their lives. Women have that same enemy, but men seem to be more vulnerable to his attacks in certain areas. Even the strongest man can get exhausted, overwhelmed, burdened, desperate, or caught up in things that keep him away from the presence of God. He doesn't always see the traps of an enemy who wants him to believe that what he faces is insurmountable. His mind fills with words like "hopeless," "no good," "failure," "impossible," "it's over," and "why try?" A wife can pray that her husband will discern the lies and hear instead words like "hope," "prosperity," "possibility," "success," and "new beginning," and know that they're from God.

The two most powerful weapons against the attack of lies upon your husband's mind are the *Word of God* and *praise*. "The Word of God is living and powerful, and sharper than any two-edged sword, piercing even to the division of soul and spirit, and of joints and marrow, and is a *discerner of the thoughts and intents of the heart*" (Hebrews 4:12). By speaking God's Word, you can reveal wrong thinking and it will lose its power. If your husband won't do it for himself, you can speak the Word of God over him, either in his presence or alone in prayer, and see positive results. I've done that for my husband countless times and he will attest to the power of it. I remind him that God has not given him a spirit of fear, but of power and of love and of a *sound mind* (2 Timothy 1:7). I tell him I'm praying for him to lay claim to that sound mind at all times.

Praise is also a powerful tool because God's presence comes to dwell in our midst when we worship Him. In His presence we find healing and transformation for our lives. "Although they knew God, they did not glorify Him as God, nor were thankful, but became futile in their thoughts, and their foolish hearts were darkened" (Romans 1:21). You don't want futile thoughts to darken your husband's heart. Speak praise to God for your husband's sound mind, and he'll be able to think more clearly about what he will and will not allow into it.

Depression, bitterness, anger, fear, rejection, hopelessness, loneliness, rebellion, temptation, evil, and many diseases all begin in the mind. These things can control your life unless you take control of your mind first. That's why God instructs us not to accept as truth everything we think. "I have stretched out My hands all day long to a rebellious people, who walk in a way that is not good, according to their own thoughts" (Isaiah 65:2). He wants us to share *His* thoughts. "We [who believe] have the mind of Christ" (1 Corinthians 2:16). Let's pray for our husbands to receive the mind of Christ and bring every thought captive under God's control. Who doesn't need that?

Prayer

Lord, I pray for Your protection on my husband's mind. Shield him from the lies of the enemy. Help him to clearly discern between Your voice and any other, and show him how to take every thought captive as You have instructed us to do. May he thirst for Your Word and hunger for Your truth so that he can recognize wrong thinking. Give him strength to resist lying thoughts. Remind him that he has the mind of Christ. Where the enemy's lies have already invaded his thoughts, I push them back by inviting the power of the Holy Spirit to cleanse his mind. Lord, You have given me authority "over all the power of the enemy" (Luke 10:19). By that authority given to me in Jesus Christ, I command all lying spirits away from my husband's mind. I proclaim that God has given (husband's name) a sound mind. He will not entertain confusion, but live in clarity. He will not be tormented with impure, evil, negative, or sinful thoughts, but be transformed by the renewing of his mind, that he may prove what is that good and acceptable and perfect will of God (Romans 12:2).

Enable him to "be strong in the Lord and in the power of His might" (Ephesians 6:10). Help him to be anxious for nothing, but in everything by prayer and supplication, with thanksgiving, let his requests be made known to You; and may Your peace, which surpasses all understanding, guard his heart and mind through Christ Jesus (Philippians 4:6,7). And finally, whatever things are true, noble, just, pure, lovely, of good report, having virtue, or anything praiseworthy, let him think on these things (Philippians 4:8).

POWER TOOLS

Though we walk in the flesh, we do not war
according to the flesh. For the weapons of our
warfare are not carnal but mighty in God for pulling
down strongholds, casting down arguments and every
high thing that exalts itself against the knowledge of
God, bringing every thought into captivity to the
obedience of Christ.
2 CORINTHIANS 10:3-5

To be carnally minded is death, but to be
spiritually minded is life and peace.
ROMANS 8:6

I see another law in my members, warring against the
law of my mind, and bringing me into captivity to
the law of sin which is in my members.
ROMANS 7:23

With the mind I myself serve the law of God,
but with the flesh the law of sin.
ROMANS 7:25

You shall love the LORD your God with all your
heart, with all your soul, with all your mind,
and with all your strength.
MARK 12:30

CHAPTER EIGHT

His Fears

here are many things in this world to be afraid of; only a fool would say otherwise. But when fear seizes us, tormenting and ruling our lives, we have become captive to it. Men are often susceptible to that because without even realizing it, they get attacked by the "what if's." "What if I can't make enough money?" "What if something happens to my wife and children?" "What if I get a terrible disease?" "What if my business fails?" "What if I can't be a good father?" "What if I become disabled and can't work to support my family?" "What if I'm overpowered or threatened?" "What if I can't perform sexually?" "What if no one respects me?" "What if I'm in an accident?" "What if I die?" Fear can take hold of a man (Psalm 48:6) and cause his life to be wasted (Psalm 78:33). If he is "seized with great fear" (Luke 8:37), it can keep him from all God has for him.

The second year we were married, Michael and I took a trip to Italy, Greece, and Israel with our pastor, Jack Hayford, and his wife, Anna, and some people from our church. Michael had always been a very anxious traveler, so by the time we arrived in Greece, he was stressed. One night, after an exhausting few days, he said, "This is miserable for me. I can't stay on the tour."

"What exactly are you afraid of?" I questioned him.

"I'm not sure," he answered. "But it feels like everything in my life is going to fall apart if I don't go back home right away."

Even though it was late in the evening, I called Pastor Jack's room to tell him we were leaving in the morning. I'm sure he must have been in bed by that time, but he said, "I'll be right there."

He came to our room immediately and Michael shared with him what he was experiencing. Pastor Jack put a compassionate arm around his shoulder and talked about the love his heavenly Father had toward him.

"God has adopted you as His son," he said. "When you're in the presence of a strong and loving Father, there's no need to be afraid."

Pastor Jack prayed for Michael to clearly perceive the love of his heavenly Father, and he also demonstrated a father's love to him. It was a simple act of Holy Spirit-inspired kindness but a powerful revelation to Michael. Because of it, he was able to rise above his fear and we stayed on the tour until the end. And it was a good thing we did. I became pregnant in Jerusalem and nine months later our son, Christopher, was born on Pastor Jack's birthday. Significant things happen in our lives when we don't allow fear to rule the situation.

There is a difference between a fearful thought that comes to mind as a prompting to pray for a particular thing, and a tormenting spirit of fear that paralyzes. You don't want to undermine the promptings of the Holy Spirit to your husband's heart, but you do want to support him as he battles destructive fear. Jesus said, "I will show you whom you should fear: Fear Him who, after He has killed, has power to cast into hell" (Luke 12:5). The only kind of fear we are supposed to have is the fear of the Lord.

When you have the fear of the Lord, God promises to deliver you from your enemies (2 Kings 17:39), protect you from evil (Proverbs 16:6), keep His eye on you (Psalm 33:18), show you His mercy (Luke 1:50), give you riches and honor (Proverbs 22:4), supply everything you need (Psalm 34:9), reveal all you need to know (Psalm 25:14), bless your children and grandchildren (Psalm 103:17), give you confidence (Proverbs 14:26), a satisfying life (Proverbs 19:23), longevity (Proverbs 10:27), and the desires of your heart (Psalm 145:19). What more could you ask? Pray for the comforting, securing, perfect love of the Lord to surround your husband and deliver him from all his fears.

Prayer

Lord, You've said in Your Word that "there is no fear in love; but perfect love casts out fear, because fear involves torment. But he who fears has not been made perfect in love" (1 John 4:18). I pray You will perfect my husband in Your love so that tormenting fear finds no place in him. I know You have not given him a spirit of fear. You've given him power, love, and a sound mind (2 Timothy 1:7). I pray in the name of Jesus that fear will not rule over my husband. Instead, may Your Word penetrate every fiber of his being, convincing him that Your love for him is far greater than anything he faces and nothing can separate him from it.

I pray that he will acknowledge You as a Father whose love is unfailing, whose strength is without equal, and in whose presence there is nothing to fear. Deliver him this day from fear that destroys and re-place it with godly fear (Jeremiah 32:40). Teach him Your way, O Lord. Help him to walk in Your truth. Unite his heart to fear Your name (Psalm 86:11). May he have no fear of men, but rise up and boldly say, "The LORD is my helper; I will not fear. What can man do to me?" (Hebrews 13:6) "How great is Your good-ness, which You have laid up for those who fear You" (Psalm 31:19).

I say to you (husband's name), "Be strong, do not fear! Behold, your God will come with vengeance, with the recompense of God; He will come and save you" (Isaiah 35:4). "In righteousness you shall be es-tablished; you shall be far from oppression, for you shall not fear" (Isaiah 54:14). "You shall not be afraid of the terror by night, nor of the arrow that flies by day, nor of the pestilence that walks in darkness, nor of the destruction that lays waste at noonday" (Psalm 91:5,6). May the Spirit of the Lord rest upon you, "the Spirit of wisdom and understanding, the Spirit of counsel and might, the Spirit of knowledge and of the fear of the LORD" (Isaiah 11:2).

POWER TOOLS

The angel of the LORD encamps all around those
who fear Him, and delivers them.
PSALM 34:7

I sought the LORD, and He heard me, and
delivered me from all my fears.
PSALM 34:4

Yea, though I walk through the valley of the
shadow of death, I will fear no evil; for You
are with me; Your rod and Your staff,
they comfort me.
PSALM 23:4

Fear not, for I am with you; be not dismayed,
for I am your God. I will strengthen you, yes,
I will help you, I will uphold you with
My righteous right hand.
ISAIAH 41:10

The LORD is my light and my salvation;
whom shall I fear? The LORD is the strength
of my life; of whom shall I be afraid?
PSALM 27:1

CHAPTER NINE

His Purpose

*E*veryone has a purpose. It's the reason we exist. It's our life's mission, objective, or plan. Generally, we're here to glorify God and do His will. How that specifically translates in our lives is unique to each of us. Your husband needs to know the reason *he* exists. He needs to be sure his life is not just an accident, but that he's here by design. He must be certain he was created for a great purpose. When he discovers that purpose, and is doing what he was created to do, becoming what he was created to be, he will find fulfillment. This can only contribute to *your* happiness as well.

If I've learned anything being married two and one half decades, it's that a wife can't put pressure on her husband to *be* something, but she can pray for him to become it. She can pray that he be molded according to God's plan and not anyone else's. Then, who he becomes will be determined by whether he hears God's call on his life or not. For God has "called us with a holy calling, not according to our works, but according to His own purpose and grace which was given to us in Christ Jesus before time began" (2 Timothy 1:9). Your husband is "predestined according to the purpose of Him who works all things according to the counsel of His will" (Ephesians 1:11,12). But you still need to pray that he hears God's call, so that who he is and what he does lines up with *God's* purpose for his life.

You can always tell when a man is not living in the purpose for which God created him. You sense his unrest. You get a feeling something is not quite right, even if you can't put your finger on what it is. When you're around a man who is fulfilling his calling and doing what he was created to do, you're aware of his inner direction, confidence, and deep security. How do you feel about what your husband is doing with his life? Do you lack peace about it because he is on a path that's unfulfilling, beating him down, or going nowhere? If so, then pray, "Lord, take my husband from this place, reveal to him what You've called him to be, and open doors to what he should be doing."

Praying that way doesn't mean your husband will be pulled out of what he's doing and dropped into something else. It *can* happen that way, but often what takes place is a change in the man's perspective. I have a friend named David, who has worked for years in a factory, making airplanes. When he heard the call of God on his life, he knew he was to help troubled teenagers in low-income families. He also knew he wasn't to leave his job to do it. As it turned out, his work provided enough money to support his family while it afforded him exactly the kind of hours he needed to do what he had to do. He has organized food distribution to needy families, free concerts for underprivileged teens, Christian outreaches for the unsaved, and peace talks between rival gangs. He has done as much to bring restoration to his strife-torn city as any one man could possibly do. His is by no means an easy job, but it is fulfilling. And he has a sense of purpose that is unmistakable when you're around him. Physically, he is not a large man, but he is a spiritual giant and you know it when you're in his presence. His wife, Priscilla, also hears God's call on his life and she supports it in every way she can.

Whatever God has called your husband to be or do, He has also called you to support it and be a part of it, if in no other way than to pray, encourage, and help in whatever way possible. For some women that means creating a good home, raising the children, being there for him, and offering prayer support. Other women may take an active role by becoming a partner or helper. In either case, God does not ask you to deny your own personhood in the process. God has called *you* to something, too. But it will fit in with whatever your husband's calling is, it will not be in conflict with it. God is not the author of confusion, strife, or unworkable situations. He is a God of perfect timing. There is a time for everything, the Bible says. The timing to do what God has called *each* of you to do will work out perfectly, if it's submitted to God.

If your husband is already moving in the purpose for which God has called him, you can count on the enemy of his soul coming to cast doubt—especially if he hasn't yet seen anything close to the finished picture or realized the success he had envisioned. Your prayers can help cast away discouragement and keep it from taking hold. It can help your husband to hear and cling to God's revelation. It can cause him to live his life on purpose.

Prayer

Lord, I pray that (husband's name) will clearly hear the call You have on his life. Help him to realize who he is in Christ and give him certainty that he was created for a high purpose. May the eyes of his understanding be enlightened so that he will know what is the hope of Your calling (Ephesians 1:18).

Lord, when You call us, You also enable us. Enable him to walk worthy of his calling and become the man of God You made him to be. Continue to remind him of what You've called him to and don't let him get sidetracked with things that are unessential to Your purpose. Strike down discouragement so that it will not defeat him. Lift his eyes above the circumstances of the moment so he can see the purpose for which You created him. Give him patience to wait for Your perfect timing. I pray that the desires of his heart will not be in conflict with the desires of Yours. May he seek You for direction, and hear when You speak to his soul.

POWER TOOLS

Each one has his own gift from God, one in
this manner and another in that.
1 CORINTHIANS 7:7

As God has distributed to each one, as the Lord
has called each one, so let him walk.
1 CORINTHIANS 7:17

We also pray always for you that our God
would count you worthy of this calling, and fulfill
all the good pleasure of His goodness and the
work of faith with power.
2 THESSALONIANS 1:11

The God of our Lord Jesus Christ, the Father of
glory, . . . give to you the spirit of wisdom and
revelation in the knowledge of Him, the eyes of
your understanding being enlightened; that you
may know what is the hope of His calling, what are
the riches of the glory of His inheritance in the
saints, and what is the exceeding greatness of His
power toward us who believe, according to the
working of His mighty power.
EPHESIANS 1:17-19

May He grant you according to your heart's
desire, and fulfill all your purpose.
PSALM 20:4

CHAPTER TEN

His Choices

*T*here was a business deal my husband entered into that he did not mention to me until it was already in motion. From the moment I learned of it I did not have a good feeling. I thought the idea was great and his vision for it was excellent, but I couldn't escape the distinct lack of peace I had about it. In fact, the more I prayed, the stronger I felt. When I mentioned it to him he said defensively, "You don't trust me to make the right decision." He made clear this was something he wanted and he was not about to hear any opposition.

The only recourse I had was to pray, which I did. Time and again I said to God, "Show me if I'm wrong about this. I would love for it to work out because it's a great idea. But if what I'm sensing is correct, reveal it to him in time to stop the process. Show him the truth and close the door."

At the eleventh hour, just before contracts were to be signed, Michael's eyes were suddenly opened to a number of incidents that called into question the true intentions of the other parties involved. The revelation of God exposed everything to him and the entire deal was called off. As hard as it was for him to accept at the time, he is grateful to have been spared much grief.

Sometime later, while I was writing this book, I asked my husband what has meant the most about my praying for him. One of the things he mentioned was that it helped him to make good choices. "When major decisions came up and I was offered certain things, your prayers opened my eyes and kept me from entering into contractual agreements that would have been bad," he explained.

We have to remember that all men think they are doing the right thing. "Every way of a man is right in his own eyes" (Proverbs 21:2). But God is the only one who can give true discernment. He can give us wisdom when we ask for it. Wisdom brings success (Ecclesiastes 10:10), and it enables us to learn from experience (Proverbs 15:31). We want our husbands to be wise men.

The opposite of a wise man is a fool. The Bible describes a fool as someone who only "trusts in his own heart" (Proverbs 28:26). He despises wisdom (Proverbs 23:9). He only wants to talk and doesn't want to listen (Proverbs 18:2). In other words, you can't tell him anything. He is quarrelsome (Proverbs 20:3), and he rages and is arrogant when you try to reason with him (Proverbs 14:16). A fool is someone who is incapable of weighing thoroughly the consequences of his actions. As a result, he doesn't make wise choices. If you have a husband like that, pray for him to have wisdom.

If your husband is not a full-time fool, so to speak, but he does occasionally engage in foolish behavior, don't try to fix him. God is the only one who can do that. Your job is to love and pray for him. The Bible says, "The fear of the LORD is the beginning of wisdom, and the knowledge of the Holy One is understanding" (Proverbs 9:10). This means you start by praying for the fear of the Lord to overtake him. Then pray for him to have godly counsel: "Blessed is the man who walks not in the counsel of the ungodly" (Psalm 1:1). If you keep praying for your husband to have wisdom and godly counsel, then even if he does make a bad decision, you can enjoy the comfort of knowing you did your part and God will bring good out of it.

So much of our lives is affected by decisions our husbands make. We are wise to pray that they make good ones.

Prayer

Lord, fill my husband with the fear of the Lord and give him wisdom for every decision he makes. May he reverence You and Your ways and seek to know Your truth. Give him discernment to make decisions based on Your revelation. Help him to make godly choices and keep him from doing anything foolish. Take foolishness out of his heart and enable him to quickly recognize error and avoid it. Open his eyes to clearly see the consequences of any anticipated behavior.

I pray that he will listen to godly counselors and not be a man who is unteachable. Give him strength to reject the counsel of the ungodly and hear Your counsel above all others. I declare that although "there are many plans in a man's heart, nevertheless the LORD's counsel—that will stand" (Proverbs 19:21). Instruct him even as he is sleeping (Psalm 16:7), and in the morning, I pray he will do what's right rather than follow the leading of his own flesh. I know the wisdom of this world is foolishness with You, Lord (1 Corinthians 3:19). May he not buy into it, but keep his eyes on You and have ears to hear Your voice.

POWER TOOLS

A wise man will hear and increase learning, and a
man of understanding will attain wise counsel.
PROVERBS 1:5

Do not be wise in your own eyes; fear the
LORD and depart from evil.
PROVERBS 3:7

The fear of the LORD is the beginning of knowledge,
but fools despise wisdom and instruction.
PROVERBS 1:7

They will call on me, but I will not answer; they will
seek me diligently, but they will not find me. Because
they hated knowledge and did not choose the fear of
the LORD, they would have none of my counsel and
despised my every rebuke.
PROVERBS 1:28-30

A man who wanders from the way of understanding
will rest in the assembly of the dead.
PROVERBS 21:16

CHAPTER ELEVEN

His Health

*F*or years my husband cared little about exercise. I would give lectures and meaningful talks, leave magazine articles in his path, and plead and cry about how I didn't want to be a widow, but it all fell on glazed eyes and deaf ears. Then one day I got the brilliant idea that if praying worked for other parts of his life, it might work for this, too. I decided to employ my "shut up and pray" method and ask God to give him the desire and motivation to exercise regularly. I prayed for a number of months without any results, but then one morning I heard an unfamiliar noise coming from another room. I followed the sound and much to my amazement, it was my husband on the treadmill. I didn't say a word. He has been using the treadmill and lifting weights about three days a week ever since. When he later remarked how much better he was feeling and wished he had started doing it sooner, I exercised admirable restraint and didn't even allow the words "I told you so" to be formed with my mouth. To this day he doesn't know I prayed.

Your husband's health is not something to take for granted, no matter what his age or condition. Pray for him to learn to take proper care of himself, and if he becomes ill, pray for him to be healed. I've seen too many answers to prayers for healing in my life and the lives of others to doubt that the God who healed in the Bible is the same yesterday, today, and tomorrow. I believe that when God said, "I am the LORD who heals You," He meant it (Exodus 15:26). I have the same faith as Jeremiah who prayed, "Heal me, O Lord, and I shall be healed" (Jeremiah 17:14). I trust His Word when it promises "I will restore health to you and heal you of your wounds" (Jeremiah 30:17).

Jesus "took our infirmities and bore our sicknesses" (Matthew 8:17). He gave His disciples power to "heal all kinds of sickness and all kinds of disease" (Matthew 10:1). He said "These signs will follow those who believe. . . . They will lay hands on the sick, and they will recover" (Mark 16:17,18). It seems to me that God is interested in healing, and He didn't put a time limit on it; only a faith limit (Matthew 9:22).

My husband told me that my prayers for his healing had the biggest impact on him in the mid-eighties when he discovered several lumps on his body and the doctor believed they were cancerous. A second doctor also suspected it was cancer, so a biopsy was taken. During those days of waiting to find out the results, Michael was tempted to worry. He said my prayers for his good health and peace sustained him until he found out it wasn't cancer at all. He had the lumps removed and there has never been a problem since.

Remember, however, that even though we pray and have faith, the outcome and timing are God's decisions. He says there is "a time to heal" (Ecclesiastes 3:3). If you pray for healing and nothing happens, don't beat yourself up for it. God sometimes uses a man's physical ailments to get his attention so He can speak to him. Keep praying, but know God's decision is the bottom line.

The same is true when praying that God will save someone's life. We don't have the final say over anyone's hour of death. The Bible says there is "a time to die" (Ecclesiastes 3:2), and we are not the ones who decide that, God does. And we must accept it. We can pray, but He determines the outcome. We have to give Him that privilege without resenting, faulting, or getting angry at Him. Pray for your husband's health, but leave it in God's hands.

Prayer

Lord, I pray for Your healing touch on (husband's name). Make every part of his body function the way You designed it to. Wherever there is anything out of balance, set it in perfect working order. Heal him of any disease, illness, injury, infirmity, or weakness. Strengthen his body to successfully endure his workload, and when he sleeps may he wake up completely rested, rejuvenated and refreshed. Give him a strong heart that doesn't fail. I don't want him to have heart failure at any time.

I pray that he will have the desire to take care of his body, to eat the kind of food that brings health, to get regular exercise, and avoid anything that would be harmful to him. Help him to understand that his body is Your temple and he should care for it as such (1 Corinthians 3:16). I pray that he will present it as a living sacrifice, holy and acceptable to You (Romans 12:1).

When he is ill, I pray You will sustain him and heal him. Fill him with your joy to give him strength. Specifically, I pray for (mention any area of concern). Give him faith to say. "'O LORD my God, I cried out to You, and You healed me' [Psalm 30:2]. Thank You, Lord, that You are my Healer." I pray that my husband will live a long and healthy life and when death does come, may it be accompanied by peace and not unbearable suffering and agony. Thank You, Lord, that You will be there to welcome him into Your presence, and not a moment before Your appointed hour.

POWER TOOLS

Bless the LORD, O my soul, and forget not all His benefits: who forgives all your iniquities, who heals all your diseases.
PSALM 103:2,3

They cried out to the LORD in their trouble, and He saved them out of their distresses. He sent His word and healed them, and delivered them from their destructions.
PSALM 107:19,20

I have heard your prayer, I have seen your tears; surely I will heal you.
2 KINGS 20:5

Your light shall break forth like the morning, your healing shall spring forth speedily, and your righteousness shall go before you; the glory of the LORD shall be your rear guard.
ISAIAH 58:8

I will heal them and reveal to them the abundance of peace and truth.
JEREMIAH 33:6

CHAPTER TWELVE

His Protection

*H*ow many times have we heard stories about men who were on the battlefield and at the very moment when they were in the greatest danger, they experienced miraculous deliverance, only to learn later that someone back home was praying at that same moment? Our husbands are on the battlefield every day. There are dangers everywhere. Only God knows what traps the enemy has laid to bring accidents, diseases, evil, violence, and destruction into our lives. Few places are completely safe anymore, including your own home. But God has said that even though "the wicked watches the righteous, and seeks to slay him, the LORD will not leave him in his hand" (Psalm 37:32,33). He promises that He will be "a shield to those who put their trust in Him" (Proverbs 30:5). He can even be a shield to someone we pray about because of *our* faith.

I have always prayed for my husband and children to be safe while traveling in cars. But one morning I got a call from Michael shortly after he left the house to take our young son to school.

"We've just had an accident," he said, "but Christopher and I are fine."

I drove immediately to where they were, thanking God all the way for protecting them just as I had prayed for years. When I arrived and saw the condition of the car, I completely fell apart. Michael's little sports car, which I was never thrilled about his driving, had been broadsided by a much larger car and pushed into a concrete barrier at the side of the road. There was so much destruction to the little car that it was later considered a total loss by the insurance company. The only way to explain why neither of them were hurt had to be the protecting hand of God. They did have bruises on their chests and shoulders from the seat belts, but they could have been injured far worse or even killed. I firmly believe that the Lord answered my prayers for protection on my family. (I'm still waiting for Him to answer the ones about my husband not buying any more sports cars.)

My prayer group and I regularly pray for our husbands to be safe in planes, cars, the workplace, or walking down the street. We don't even have to think of all the specific dangers, we just ask the Lord to protect them from harm. God promises to "give His angels charge over you, to keep you in all your ways. In their hands they shall bear you up, lest you dash your foot against a stone" (Psalm 91:11,12). But accidents do happen, even to godly people, and when they do they are sudden and unexpected. That's why prayer for your husband's protection needs to be frequent and ongoing. You never know when it might be needed in the battlefield. And if something happens, you'll have the comfort of knowing you've invited God's presence and power into the midst of it.

Prayer

Lord, I pray that You would protect (husband's name) from any accidents, diseases, dangers, or evil influences. Keep him safe, especially in cars and planes. Hide him from violence and the plans of evil people. Wherever he walks, secure his steps. Keep him on Your path so that his feet don't slip (Psalm 17:5). If his foot does slip, hold him up by Your mercy (Psalm 94:18). Give him the wisdom and discretion that will help him walk safely and not fall into danger (Proverbs 3:21-23). Be his fortress, strength, shield, and stronghold (Psalm 18:2,3). Make him to dwell in the shadow of Your wings (Psalm 91:1-2). Be his rock, salvation, and defense, so that he will not be moved or shaken (Psalm 62:6). I pray that even though bad things may be happening all around him, they will not come near him (Psalm 91:7). Save him from any plans of the enemy that seek to destroy his life (Psalm 103:4). Preserve his going out and his coming in from this time forth and even forevermore (Psalm 121:8).

POWER TOOLS

He who dwells in the secret place of the Most High shall abide under the shadow of the Almighty. I will say of the LORD, "He is my refuge and my fortress; my God, in Him I will trust."
PSALM 91:1-2

In the time of trouble He shall hide me in His pavilion; in the secret place of His tabernacle He shall hide me; He shall set me high upon a rock.
PSALM 27:5

Yea, though I walk through the valley of the shadow
of death, I will fear no evil; for You are with me; Your
rod and Your staff, they comfort me.

PSALM 23:4

The LORD is my rock and my fortress and my
deliverer; my God, my strength, in whom I will trust;
my shield and the horn of my salvation, my stronghold. I will call upon the LORD, who is worthy to be
praised; so shall I be saved from my enemies.

PSALM 18:2,3

Show Your marvelous lovingkindness by Your right
hand, O You who save those who trust in You from
those who rise up against them. Keep me as the apple
of Your eye; hide me under the shadow of Your wings.

PSALM 17:7,8

CHAPTER THIRTEEN

His Trials

*E*veryone goes through hard times. It's nothing to be ashamed of. Sometimes our prayers help us to avoid them. Sometimes not. It's the attitude we have when we go through them that matters most. If we are filled with anger and bitterness, or insist on complaining and blaming God, things tend to turn out badly. If we go through them with thankfulness and praise to God, He promises to bring good things despite them. He says to "count it all joy when you fall into various trials, knowing that the testing of your faith produces patience" (James 1:2,3).

A wife's prayers for her husband during these times may not change some of the things he must go through. After all, if we never suffered anything, what kind of shallow, compassionless, impatient people would we be? But prayer can help him maintain a positive outlook of gratitude, hope, patience, and peace in the midst of it, and keep him from reaping the penalty of a wrong response.

My friend, Jan, watched her husband, Dave, hover near death as a result of being bitten by a poisonous spider. It was a terrifying time for both of them and the trial lasted for well over a year as he struggled to rise above each new physical problem that happened as a result. On top of that they had just moved to a new state, away from family, friends, and church, and they suffered financially because of the enormous medical bills. There was every reason to be angry and bitter, but they never allowed themselves to stop praying, praising God, and looking to Him as their source.

Through countless tears and fears of her own, Jan fervently prayed that Dave would not get discouraged in the battle, but be able to stand strong through it. God sustained them, Dave did recover, and they have become two of the richest people in the Lord one could ever hope to meet. Not only that, but their three children are all strong believers who use their enormous talents to glorify God. Dave became a music pastor at a church where he and Jan now have a highly successful ministry. Their lives are a testimony to the goodness of the Lord, and I believe that the manner in which they went through this trial has a lot to do with where they are today.

Whether it feels like it or not, when we serve God, His love attends every moment of our lives—even the toughest, loneliest, most painful and desperate. He is always there in our midst, working things out for good when we pray and look to Him to do so. "We know that all things work together for good to those who love God, to those who are the called according to His purpose" (Romans 8:28). His purpose for our trials is often to bring us humbly before Him to experience a breaking in our inner, independent, self-sufficient selves, and grow us up into compassionate, patient, spiritually strong, God-glorifying people. He uses these situations to teach us how to trust that He loves and cares for us enough to get us through the tough times.

I can't think of any trial that my husband or I have gone through that didn't grow us deeper in the things of God, even though it was miserable to endure at the time and we had little appreciation of where we were headed. But as we prayed through every rough spot, we found our faith growing and our walk with God deepening. And when our attitudes were right, so did our love for one another.

If your husband is going through a difficult time, carry it in prayer, but don't carry the burden. Even though you may want to, don't try to take away his load and make it yours. That will ultimately leave him feeling weak or like a failure. Besides, God doesn't want you doing *His* job. He doesn't want you trying to be the Holy Spirit to your husband. Even though it hurts to see him struggle and you want to fix it, you can't. You can pray, encourage, and support, but God uses trials for His purpose and you must stay out of His way.

If your husband feels crushed under the weight of such things as financial strain, illness, disability, loss of work, problems with the children, marital strife, catastrophes, disasters in the home, or strained relationships, invite the Holy Spirit to move into his circumstances and transform them. Remind your husband of the bigger picture: our suffering will seem like nothing compared to the glory of God worked in us, if we have the right reactions in the midst of the struggle. "For I consider that the sufferings of this present time are not worthy to be compared with the glory which shall be revealed in us" (Romans 8:18). Encourage him to say, "I can do all things through Christ who strengthens me" (Philippians 4:13).

Pray that your husband will be able to press in closer to God until he knows that nothing can separate him from His love—not what he is going through now and not what will happen in the future. "For I am persuaded that neither death nor life, nor angels nor principalities nor powers, nor things present nor things to come, nor height nor depth, nor any other created thing, shall be able to separate us from the love of God which is in Christ Jesus our Lord" (Romans 8:38,39). If nothing can separate him from the love of God, then no matter how bad it gets, he always has hope.

Trials can be a purifying fire and a cleansing water. You don't want your husband to get burned or drowned; you want him to get refined and renewed. God has promised that "in all these things we are more than conquerors through Him who loved us" (Romans 8:37). "He who endures to the end shall be saved" (Matthew 24:13). It's the determination of your husband to stand strong in faith and wait for God to answer his prayers that will save him from the heat and keep him afloat.

Prayer

Lord, You alone know the depth of the burden my husband carries. I may understand the specifics, but You have measured the weight of it on his shoulders. I've not come to minimize what You are doing in his life, for I know You work great things in the midst of trials. Nor am I trying to protect him from what he must face. I only want to support him so that he will get through this battle as the winner.

God, You are our refuge and strength, a very present help in trouble (Psalm 46:1). You have invited us to "come boldly to the throne of grace, that we may obtain mercy and find grace to help in time of need" (Hebrews 4:16). I come before Your throne and ask for grace for my husband. Strengthen his heart for this battle and give him patience to wait on You (Psalm 27:1-4). Build him up so that no matter what happens he will be able to stand strong through it. Help him to be always "rejoicing in hope, patient in tribulation, continuing steadfastly in prayer" (Romans 12:12). Give him endurance to run the race and not give up, for You have said that "a righteous man may fall seven times and rise again" (Proverbs 24:16). Help him to remember that "the steps of a good man are ordered by the LORD, and He delights in his way. Though he fall, he shall not be utterly cast down; for the LORD upholds him with His hand" (Psalm 37:23,24).

I pray he will look to You to be his "refuge until these calamities have passed by" (Psalm 57:1). May he learn to wait on You because "those who wait on the LORD shall renew their strength; they shall mount up with wings like eagles, they shall run and not be weary, they shall walk and not faint" (Isaiah 40:31). I pray that he will find his strength in You and as he cries out to You, You will hear him and save him out of all his troubles (Psalm 34:6).

POWER TOOLS

You have been grieved by various trials, that the genuineness of your faith, being much more precious than gold that perishes, though it is tested by fire, may be found to praise, honor, and glory at the revelation of Jesus Christ.

1 PETER 1:6,7

Cast your burden on the LORD, and He shall
sustain you; He shall never permit the
righteous to be moved.
PSALM 55:22

As for me, I will call upon God, and the LORD shall
save me. Evening and morning and at noon I will
pray, and cry aloud, and He shall hear my voice. He
has redeemed my soul in peace from the battle
that was against me.
PSALM 55:16-18

You, who have shown me great and severe troubles,
shall revive me again, and bring me up again from
the depths of the earth. You shall increase my greatness, and comfort me on every side.
PSALM 71:20,21

CHAPTER FOURTEEN

His Integrity

Integrity is not what you *appear* to be when all eyes are on you. It's who you *are* when no one is looking. It's a level of morality below which you never fall, no matter what's happening around you. It's a high standard of honesty, truthfulness, decency, and honor that is never breached. It's doing for others the way you would want them to do for you.

A man of integrity says something and means it. He doesn't play verbal games so you never really know where he stands. He knows to let his "Yes" be "Yes" and his "No" be "No." "For whatever is more than these is from the evil one" (Matthew 5:37). He will not play both sides of the fence to please everyone. His goal is to please God and do what is right. A man can be highly esteemed among men but an abomination to God (Luke 16:15).

A man of integrity "swears to his own hurt and does not change" (Psalm 15:4). He will keep his word even if it costs him something to do so. When placed in a possibly compromising situation, he will continue to stand strong in what he believes. Above all, he is a man of truth; you can depend on his solid honesty. A man "who walks with integrity walks securely" (Proverbs 10:9), because his integrity guides him and brings him into the presence of God (Psalm 41:12).

My husband is a man of integrity who has had to take a stand a number of times against things he believed were wrong. It often cost him a great deal. I've always prayed for him to do the right thing, but not because he wouldn't have done it without me. He surely would have. However, my prayers supported him as he faced opposition and helped him to stand strong through it. The Bible says, "The righteous man walks in his integrity; his children are blessed after him" (Proverbs 20:7). Whether my children fully recognize it or not, they will receive a heritage from their father's adherence to the principles of high moral integrity. There are blessings they will enjoy because of the kind of man he is. I pray they will pass those on to *their* children.

Integrity happens in the heart. Therefore, being a man of integrity is something your husband must *choose* to do on his own. But you can prayerfully help him fight the enemy that seeks to snare him, blind him, and keep him from making that decision. Even when he makes the right choice, there will be a negative reaction to it in the realm of evil. Your prayers can help shield him from anything that causes him to doubt and waver, and give him strength to do what's right—even when no one's looking.

Prayer

Lord, I pray that You would make my husband a man of integrity, according to Your standards. Give him strength to say "Yes" when he should say "Yes," and courage to say "No" when he should say "No." Enable him to stand for what he knows is right and not waver under pressure from the world. Don't let him be a man who is "always learning and never able to come to a knowledge of the truth" (2 Timothy 3:7). Give him, instead, a teachable spirit that is willing to listen to the voice of wisdom and grow in Your ways.

Make him a man who lives by truth. Help him to walk with Your Spirit of truth at all times (John 16:13). Be with him to bear witness to the truth so that in times of pressure he will act on it with confidence (1 John 1:8,9). Where he has erred in this and other matters, give him a heart that is quick to confess his mistakes. For You have said in Your Word, "If we say that we have no sin, we deceive ourselves, and the truth is not in us. If we confess our sins, He is faithful and just to forgive us our sins and to cleanse us from all unrighteousness" (1 John 1:8,9). Don't let him be deceived. Don't let him live a lie in any way. Bind mercy and truth around his neck and write them on the tablet of his heart so he will find favor and high esteem in the sight of God and man (Proverbs 3:3,4).

POWER TOOLS

Better is the poor who walks in his integrity than one perverse in his ways, though he be rich.
PROVERBS 28:6

The integrity of the upright will guide them, but the perversity of the unfaithful will destroy them.
PROVERBS 11:3

Judge me, O Lord, according to my righteousness,
and according to my integrity within me.
Psalm 7:8

Vindicate me, O Lord, for I have walked in my
integrity. I have also trusted in the Lord;
I shall not slip.
Psalm 26:1

Let integrity and uprightness preserve me,
for I wait for You.
Psalm 25:21

CHAPTER FIFTEEN

His Reputation

A good reputation is a fragile thing, especially in this day of rapid communication and mass media. Just being in the wrong place at the wrong time can ruin a person's life.

A reputation is not something to be taken lightly. A good name is to be chosen over great riches (Proverbs 22:1) and is better than the "precious ointment" (Ecclesiastes 7:1). It's something to value and protect. A person who doesn't value his reputation may someday desire credibility and not find it. Our reputations can be ruined by wrong things we do, by the people with whom we are associated, or by disparaging words spoken about us. In all three cases, evil is involved. One unfortunate court case, a significant round of gossip, an evil influence, an unflattering newspaper article, or fifteen minutes of notoriety can destroy everything a man has worked for all his life. Prayer is our only defense.

The times my husband was most concerned about his reputation was when he or someone else had been misquoted in a newspaper article as saying something that wasn't true. Because we knew how damaging these kinds of things can be, we always called people we thought would be most affected by any misquotes and told them what the truth was. Of course we couldn't possibly call everyone, so we prayed that those we did call would be enough and that God would put an end to it. As it turned out, what could have been wildfires totally burned themselves out within a day or two. It could easily have gone the other way and consumed us. I am certain it was the power of God in response to prayer that kept us protected.

A virtuous wife, the Bible says, has a husband who is respected. He is "known in the gates, when he sits among the elders of the land" (Proverbs 31:23). Does that just happen? Is every virtuous wife guaranteed a husband with a good reputation? Or does she have something to do with that? It's true that a man gets a certain amount of respect for having a good wife, but I believe one of the good things she does is pray for him and his reputation.

Prayer for your husband's reputation should be an ongoing process. However, keep in mind that he has a free will. If he is not sensitive to the leading of the Holy Spirit, he may still choose to go his own way and get into trouble. If something like that happens or has already happened to tarnish his reputation, pray for God to redeem the situation and bring good out of it. He can do that, too.

Prayer

Lord, I pray that (husband's name) will have a reputation that is untarnished. I know that a man is often valued "by what others say of him" (Proverbs 27:21), so I pray that he will be respected in our town and people will speak highly of him.

You've said in Your Word that "a curse without cause shall not alight" (Proverbs 26:2). I pray that there would never be any reason for bad things to be said of him. Keep him out of legal entanglements. Protect us from lawsuits and criminal proceedings. Deliver him from his enemies, O God. Defend him from those who rise up to do him harm (Psalm 59:1). Fight against those who fight against him (Psalm 35:1). In You, O Lord, we put our trust. Let us never be put to shame (Psalm 71:1). If You are for us, who can be against us (Romans 8:31)?

Your Word says that "a good tree cannot bear bad fruit, nor can a bad tree bear good fruit. Every tree that does not bear good fruit is cut down and thrown into the fire" (Matthew 7:18,19). I pray that my husband will bear good fruit out of the goodness that is within him, and that he will be known by the good that he does. May the fruits of honesty, trustworthiness, and humility sweeten all his dealings so that his reputation will never be spoiled.

Preserve his life from the enemy, hide him from the secret counsel of the wicked. Pull him out of any net which has been laid for him (Psalm 31:4). Keep him safe from the evil of gossiping mouths. Where there has been ill spoken of him, touch the lips of those who speak it with Your refining fire. Let the responsibility of those involved be revealed. Let them be ashamed and brought to confusion who seek to destroy his life; let them be driven backward and brought to dishonor who wish him evil (Psalm 40:14). May he trust in You and not be afraid of what man can do to

him (Psalm 56:11). For You have said whoever believes in You will not be put to shame (Romans
10:11). Lead him, guide him, and be his mighty
fortress and hiding place. May his light so shine before
men that they see his good works and glorify You, Lord
(Matthew 5:16).

POWER TOOLS

Hide me from the secret plots of the wicked, from
the rebellion of the workers of iniquity, who sharpen
their tongue like a sword, and bend their bows to
shoot their arrows—bitter words.
PSALM 64:2,3

Do not let me be ashamed, O LORD, for I have called
upon You; let the wicked be ashamed; let them be
silent in the grave. Let the lying lips be put to
silence, which speak insolent things proudly and
contemptuously against the righteous.
PSALM 31:17,18

Blessed are you when they revile and persecute you,
and say all kinds of evil against you falsely for My
sake. Rejoice and be exceedingly glad, for great is
your reward in heaven, for so they persecuted the
prophets who were before you.
MATTHEW 5:11,12

Do not go hastily to court; for what will you do in
the end, when your neighbor has put you to shame?
Debate your case with your neighbor, and do not dis-
close the secret to another; lest he who hears it
expose your shame, and your reputation be ruined.
PROVERBS 25:8-10

Who shall bring a charge against God's elect? It is
God who justifies. Who is he who condemns?
It is Christ who died, and furthermore is also risen,
who is even at the right hand of God, who also
makes intercession for us.

ROMANS 8:33,34

CHAPTER SIXTEEN

His Priorities

*M*en have many different ideas about what their priorities should be. But every wife feels she should be at the top of her husband's list—right there under God. I've found, however, that if a wife wants her husband's priorities to be in that kind of order, she has to make sure *hers* are in that order as well. In other words, if you want your husband to place you as a priority over work, children, friends, and activities, you need to do the same for him. If God and spouse aren't clearly top priorities in *your* life, your husband will have less incentive to make them so in his.

I know very well about the struggle to keep a right order of priorities, especially if there are little ones in the picture. Children's needs are immediate and urgent and you're the one to take care of them. A husband, after all, is an adult and hopefully can take care of himself. Even if there are no children, it's possible to be consumed by work, home, friends, projects, interests, and activities. It's hard, in the midst of everything that occupies your time and attention, not to allow your husband to fall down on the list—or at least feel as though he has.

Fortunately, priorities don't always have to do with the total amount of time spent on them, otherwise anyone with a forty-hour work week would be putting God second to their job unless he or she was praying at least eight hours a day. And there is no way a wife can give as much time to her husband as she does to a young child without neglecting the child. When it comes to your husband, it's not so much a matter of how much time you take, but that you *do* take time to make him feel like he is a priority.

Just greeting him first thing in the morning with a smile and a hug can make him feel he's important to you. So is asking him, "Is there anything you want me to do for you today?" (And then when he tells you, remember to do it.) Also, let him know you are praying for him and ask what he specifically wants you to pray about. Even checking in with him periodically in the midst of the many other things you are doing assures him he's still at the top of your list.

Priorities have to do with the position in the heart. Planning times for just the two of you—a date, a night or two away, a dinner alone, time in the home without any children or friends—communicates to him that he is a priority in your heart. If you want your husband to love *you* more, you need to love *him* more. It always works, especially if you're praying about it as well.

If you feel that you just don't have the time and energy to put your husband first and still do all that's expected of you, ask God for a fresh filling of His Holy Spirit. Seek Him first and He will help you get your priorities in order. If your schedule doesn't allow time to be with God and draw on His strength, then rework your priorities and make a new schedule. The old one is not working.

In the business my husband is in, we often see people experience success quickly. The problem with that is a spirit of lust for *more* success, *more* power, and *more* wealth usually comes along with it. When these people don't make a special effort to keep their priorities in order, their pride guides them, and they buy into its lure. They slip into overdrive, leaving God, family, church, and friends in their dust. When these shooting stars come back to earth, the landing is often hard. We don't want that to happen, even on a small scale, to our husbands. Pray for your husband to always put God first, you second, and children third. Then, no matter what else is going on in his life, his priorities will be in order and there will be greater peace and happiness ahead for both of you.

Prayer

God, I proclaim You Lord over my life. Help me to seek You first every day and set my priorities in perfect order. Reveal to me how to properly put my husband before children, work, family, friends, activities, and interests. Show me what I can do right now to demonstrate to him that he has this position in my heart. Mend the times I have caused him to doubt that. Tell me how to prioritize everything so that whatever steals life away, or has no lasting purpose, will not occupy my time.

I pray for my husband's priorities to be in perfect order as well. Be Lord and Ruler over his heart. Help him to choose a simplicity of life that will allow him to have time alone with You, Lord, a place to be quiet in Your presence every day. Speak to him about making Your Word, prayer, and praise a priority. Enable him to place me and our children in greater prominence in his heart than career, friends, and activities. I pray he will seek You first and submit his all to You, for when he does I know the other pieces of his life will fit together perfectly.

POWER TOOLS

Seek first the kingdom of God and His
righteousness, and all these things shall
be added to you.
MATTHEW 6:33

Let each of you look out not only for his own
interests, but also for the interests of others.
PHILIPPIANS 2:4

No one can serve two masters; for either he will hate
the one and love the other, or else he will be loyal to
the one and despise the other.
MATTHEW 6:24

The kingdom of heaven is like a merchant seeking
beautiful pearls, who, when he had found one
pearl of great price, went and sold all that he
had and bought it.
MATTHEW 13:45,46

You shall worship the LORD your God, and Him
only you shall serve.
MATTHEW 4:10

CHAPTER SEVENTEEN

His Relationships

solation is not healthy. We all need the influence of good people to keep us on the right path. Every married couple should have at least two strong believing couples with whom they can share encouragement, strength, and the richness of their lives. Being around such people is edifying, enriching, balancing, and fulfilling, and it helps us keep perspective when things seem to grow out of proportion. Having the positive qualities of other people rub off on us is the best thing for a marriage.

I remember one time when Michael and I had an argument just before we were to be at another couple's house for dinner. On the drive there we sat in stiffened silence, and all I could think about was how we could possibly get through the evening gracefully without making the other couple very uncomfortable. When we arrived, the warmth, love, and rich godliness we felt from them infected our thoughts and emotions. Soon we were laughing and talking and having a great time, forgetting about what had transpired previously. What those two people had was not just a "let the good times roll" party spirit. It was the joy of the Lord, and it wore off on us.

We've witnessed the exact same thing happen in reverse. There have been numerous instances when a couple in the midst of marital strife came to our house for dinner and went away with peace in their hearts. One particular couple even called just before they were to arrive—when the dinner was completely ready—to say that they'd just had a bad argument and couldn't possibly be enjoyable guests. I told them we completely understood, having experienced the same thing ourselves, but that we wanted them to come, even if they sat in silence all night. "Besides, you do need to eat," I said. "If necessary you can sit at opposite ends of the table." It took some persuading, but they came and it turned out to be a highly enjoyable evening for all. We even ended up laughing about what transpired earlier and they left hand in hand.

Being good friends with godly people who love the Lord doesn't just happen by chance. We must pray that such people will come into our lives. And then when we find them, we should continue to cover the relationships in prayer. We should also pray the bad influences away. The Bible says we must "not be unequally yoked together with unbelievers" (2 Corinthians 6:14). This doesn't mean we can never be around anyone who isn't a Christian, but our closest, most influential relationships should be with people who know and love the Lord, or there will be consequences. "The righteous should choose his friends carefully, for the way of the wicked leads them astray" (Proverbs 12:26). That's why it's very important to have a church home where it's possible to meet the kind of people you need. Choose to be around the highest quality people you can, the ones whose hearts are aimed toward God.

Pray also for your husband to have godly male friends. And when he finds them, give him time to be with them without criticism. Those friends will refine him. "As iron sharpens iron, so a man sharpens the countenance of his friend" (Proverbs 27:17). They will be a good influence. "Ointment and perfume delight the heart, and the sweetness of a man's friend does so by hearty counsel" (Proverbs 27:9). Of course if it becomes obsessive, pray for balance.

After we had children, Michael worked every day and night during the week and on the weekends he spent all his spare time on the golf course or at baseball and football games with his friends. There were many bitter arguments about that, but no changes happened until I started praying that *God* would convict him and turn his heart toward home. God did a much better job than I ever could have.

Often men have fewer close friends than women because of the way their time is consumed with establishing their careers. They don't take the necessary steps to develop close friendships like we do. That's where prayer can make a difference. Even if your husband is not a believer, you can still pray for him to have godly friends. A close friend of mine has a husband who doesn't know the Lord and we have prayed many times for him to have godly friends and be in contact with believers where he works. God has now brought so many strong Christians into his life that we laugh about how the Lord has him surrounded.

Pray about *all* of your husband's relationships. He needs to have good relationships with his parents, brothers, sisters, aunts, uncles, cousins, coworkers, and neighbors. Pray that none of his relationships be marred by his inability to forgive. A husband who is tortured with unforgiveness is not a pretty sight.

Prayer

Lord, I pray for (husband's name) to have good, godly male friends with whom he can openly share his heart. May they be trustworthy men of wisdom who will speak truth into his life and not just say what he wants to hear (Proverbs 28:23). Give him the discernment to separate himself from anyone who will not be a good influence (1 Corinthians 5:13). Show him the importance of godly friendships and help me encourage him to sustain them. Give us believing married couples with whom we can feel comfortable sharing our lives.

I pray for strong, peaceful relationships with each of his family members, neighbors, acquaintances, and coworkers. Today I specifically pray for his relationship with (name of person). Inspire open communication and mutual acceptance between them. Let there be reconciliation where there has been estrangement. Work peace into anything that needs to be worked out.

I pray that in his heart he will honor his father and mother so that he will live long and be blessed in his life (Exodus 20:12). Enable him to be a forgiving person and not carry grudges or hold things in his heart against others. Lord, You've said in Your Word that "he who hates his brother is in darkness and walks in darkness, and does not know where he is going, because the darkness has blinded his eyes" (1 John 2:11). I pray that my husband would never be blinded by the darkness of unforgiveness, but continually walk in the light of forgiveness. May he not judge or show contempt for anyone but remember that "we shall all stand before the judgment seat of Christ" (Romans 14:10). Enable him to love his enemies, bless those who curse him, do good to those who hate him, and pray for those who spitefully use him and persecute him (Matthew 5:44). I pray that I will be counted as his best friend and that our friendship with one another will continue to grow. Show him what it means to be a true friend and enable him to be one.

POWER TOOLS

Let us consider one another in order to stir up love and good works, not forsaking the assembling of ourselves together, as is the manner of some, but exhorting one another.
HEBREWS 10:24,25

If you bring your gift to the altar, and there remember that your brother has something against you, leave your gift there before the altar, and go your way. First be reconciled to your brother, and then come and offer your gift.
MATTHEW 5:23,24

If we walk in the light as He is in the light, we have fellowship with one another.
1 JOHN 1:7

Take heed to yourselves. If your brother sins against you, rebuke him; and if he repents, forgive him. And if he sins against you seven times in a day, and seven times in a day returns to you, saying, "I repent," you shall forgive him.
LUKE 17:3,4

A new commandment I give to you, that you love one another; as I have loved you, that you also love one another. By this all will know that you are My disciples, if you have love for one another.

JOHN 13:34,35

CHAPTER EIGHTEEN

His Fatherhood

*W*hen I asked my husband to share with me his deepest fears, one of the things he mentioned was the fear of not being a good father. "I believe it's something men in general tend to fear," he said. "We get so caught up in doing what we do in our work that we're afraid we haven't done enough with our children. Or we're afraid we haven't done it *well* enough, or we're missing something. It becomes even more of a problem with teenagers. We fear we can't communicate with them because we'll be perceived as old and irrelevant."

I was touched by his perspective and resolved to pray for him to be a good father. I believe my prayers made a difference because I saw him become more patient with our children and less insecure about his own parenting skills. He grew increasingly relaxed and able to enjoy them. He became less guilt-ridden or angry when it was necessary to discipline them and more able to speak wisdom powerfully into their lives. He now sees that any flaw in our children is not necessarily a reflection of his value as a father.

Thoughts of failure and inadequacy are what cause so
many fathers to give up, leave, become overbearing from
trying too hard, or develop a passive attitude and fade into
the background of their children's lives. It can be especially
overwhelming to a man who already feels like a failure in
other areas. Mothers get overwhelmed with feelings of inadequacy, too, but only the most deeply disturbed ever
abandon, ignore, or hurt their children. That's because we
have the opportunity from the moment of conception to
pour so much of ourselves into our children's lives. We carry
them in the womb, we nurse and nurture them as newborns,
we guide and teach and love them so much that we have a
full sense of bonding from the start. Fathers don't have that
privilege and often feel they are starting on the outside, trying
to work their way in. If they are also spending a great amount
of time and energy trying to establish their careers, they can
easily feel hopelessly removed and ineffectual. Our prayers
can help redeem this situation.

Have you ever had someone pray for you when you
couldn't think straight, and after they prayed you had complete clarity and vision? I've experienced that countless
times. I believe this is what can happen for our husbands
when we pray about their parenting. If they are tortured with
doubt and burdened by a sense of responsibility, we can minimize these feelings with our prayers. Prayer can help them
gain a clear perspective of what it means to be a good father,
and open the door to Holy Spirit guidance on how to handle
the parenting challenges that arise.

My husband recalled a specific incident where he knew
my prayers for him regarding his fatherhood had made a big
difference. It happened when our son, Christopher, was about
seven and we had caught him in a lie. We knew we had to
deal with it, but we wanted a full confession from him along

with a repentant heart. Neither was forthcoming at that moment. Michael wanted to teach him a lesson but didn't know what to do, so he asked me to pray. While I was praying, it became very clear to him. As Chris watched, Michael drew a triangle and a picture of Satan, God, and Christopher, one at each of the points. He then described Satan's plan for Chris, and God's plan for Chris. He illustrated how lying was part of Satan's plan that Chris was going along with. He described in detail the ultimate consequences of going along with Satan's plans—which meant traveling on a spectrum away from God—and it shook Christopher up so badly that he broke down and confessed the lie with a completely repentant heart. Michael said he knew that without that clear picture from God he would not have been able to get through to his son with the depth he needed to.

The best way for a man to be a good father is to get to know his heavenly Father and learn to imitate Him. The more time he spends in the Lord's presence, being transformed into His likeness, the better influence he will be when he spends time with his children. He will have a father's heart because he understands *The Father's* heart. This can be difficult if your husband didn't have a good relationship with his earthly father. The way a man relates to his dad will often affect how he relates to his Father God. If he was abandoned by him, he may fear being abandoned by God. If his father was distant or uncaring, he may see God as distant and uncaring. If he doubted his father's love, he may doubt his heavenly Father's love. If he is angry with his father, he may be angry with his Father God as well. Events of the past with regard to his own dad can serve as a barrier that keeps him from truly knowing the Father's love. This will carry over into his relationship with his children.

Pray that your husband grows into a greater understanding of his heavenly Father's love and be healed of any misconceptions he has in his heart and mind about it. Where his father has failed him and he has blamed God, ask the Lord to heal that enormous hurt. The Bible says, "Whoever curses his father or his mother, his lamp will be put out in deep darkness" (Proverbs 20:20). Unless for-giveness happens in his heart for his dad, he will be in the dark as to how to be the best father for his children. His father doesn't have to be alive in order to right that rela-tionship, because it's what is in his own heart regarding his dad that matters. Pray that he will gain a right attitude toward his earthly father so nothing will stand in the way of his relationship with his Father God.

Men don't always realize how important they are to their children. They sometimes feel they are only there to provide materially for them. But the importance of a father's influence can never be underestimated. How he relates to his children will shape their lives for bad or for good. It will change *his* life forever, too. For if he fails as a father, he will always carry that sense of failure with him. If he succeeds, there will be no greater measure of success in his life.

Prayer

Lord, teach (husband's name) to be a good father. Where it was not modeled to him according to Your ways, heal those areas and help him to forgive his dad. Give him revelation of You and a hunger in his heart to really know You as his heavenly Father. Draw him close to spend time in Your presence so he can become more like You, and fully understand Your Father's heart of compassion and love toward him. Grow that same heart in him for his children. Help him to balance mercy, judgment, and instruction the way You do. Though You require obedience, You are quick to acknowledge a repentant heart. Make him that way, too. Show him when to discipline and how. Help him to see that he who loves his child disciplines him promptly (Proverbs 13:24). May he never provoke his "children to wrath, but bring them up in the training and admonition of the Lord" (Ephesians 6:4). I pray we will be united in the rules we set for our children and be in full agreement as to how they are raised. I pray that there will be no strife or argument over how to handle them and the issues that surround their lives.

Give him skills of communication with his children. I pray he will not be stern, hard, cruel, cold, abusive, noncommunicative, passive, critical, weak, uninterested, neglectful, undependable, or uninvolved. Help him instead to be kind, loving, softhearted, warm, interested, affirming, affectionate, involved, strong, consistent, dependable, verbally communicative, understanding, and patient. May he require and inspire his children to honor him as their father so that their lives will be long and blessed.

Lord, I know we pass a spiritual inheritance to our children. Let the heritage he passes on be one rich in the fullness of Your Holy Spirit. Enable him to model clearly a walk of submission to Your laws. May he delight in his children and long to grow them up Your way. Being a good father is something he wants very much. I pray that You would give him the desire of his heart.

POWER TOOLS

Children's children are the crown of old men, and
the glory of children is their father.
PROVERBS 17:6

For whom the LORD loves He corrects, just as a father the son in whom he delights.
PROVERBS 3:12

The father of the righteous will greatly rejoice, and
he who begets a wise child will delight in him.
PROVERBS 23:24

Correct your son, and he will give you rest; yes, he
will give delight to your soul.
PROVERBS 29:17

I will be a Father to you, and you shall be My sons
and daughters, says the LORD Almighty.
2 CORINTHIANS 6:18

CHAPTER NINETEEN

His Past

*M*ichael was nineteen when he collapsed from nervous exhaustion. He was attending college full time during the day and writing, arranging, playing piano and drums in local clubs in the afternoons and evenings. He had high stress, little sleep, and was rapidly working himself to death. The family doctor suggested he be placed in a nearby mental hospital where he could get the rest he needed. His mother later told me that she *and* the doctor regretted that decision, but at the time they didn't know what else to do. Michael described his two weeks of "rest" there as the most frightening experience of his life. He observed so much strange and horrifying behavior in the other patients that it traumatized him with fear that he might never get out. He went back to college with a less-stressful work schedule, but also great fear.

Throughout the years we've been married, there have been times when he was so overworked and pressured that he experienced that same kind of exhaustion. It always reminded him of what had happened when he was a teenager.

The past would come upon him like a specter and threaten him with the thought, *You're going to end up in a mental hospital again*. It's been at those times, he said, that my prayers for him have meant the most. I always prayed that he would know the truth, and the truth would set him free (John 8:32). I prayed for God to deliver him from his past. This has been a gradual process, but I saw strides forward every time I prayed.

The past should not be a place where we live, but something from which we learn. We are to forget "those things which are behind" and reach "forward to those things which are ahead," and we're to "press toward the goal for the prize of the upward call of God in Christ Jesus" (Philippians 3:13,14). God is a redeemer and a restorer. We need to allow Him to be both. He can redeem the past and restore what was lost. He can make up for the bad things that have happened (Psalm 90:15). We must trust Him to do those things. We can never move out of the present into the future of what God has for us if we cling to and live in the past.

Your husband's past not only affects him, it affects your offspring as well. More is passed down to your children and grandchildren than just the color of your hair and eyes. We can leave a legacy as painful and damaging as the one we experienced ourselves. We can bequeath a heritage of divorce, anger, anxiety, depression, and fear, to name a few. Whatever you and your husband can free yourselves from will mean more freedom for them. As long as you dwell in the past, you not only lose some of what God has for your future, but for your children's future as well.

The events of your husband's past that most affect his life today probably occurred in his childhood. Bad things that happened or good things that *didn't* happen with family members are the most significant. Being labeled in a certain way by a relative or peer carries over into adulthood. Such words as "fat," "stupid," "uncoordinated," "failure," "poor," "loser," "slob," "four-eyes," "slow," or "idiot" take their toll and imprint themselves into the mind and emotions well into adulthood. While no one can pretend the past didn't happen, it's possible to pray that all the effects of it are removed. No one is destined to live with them forever.

God says we are to cry out for deliverance, walk in His ways, proclaim His truth, and then we will find freedom from our past. But sometimes there are *levels* of freedom to go through. Your husband may think he's gotten free of something and it will rear its head again, leaving him feeling like he's right back where he started. Tell him not to be discouraged by that. If he has been walking with the Lord, he is probably moving into a deeper level of liberty that God wants to work in his life. Your prayers will surely gird him for the journey to greater freedom.

Being set free from the past can happen quickly or it can be a step-by-step process, depending on what God is teaching. The problem is, you can't make it happen on your timetable. You have to be patient and pray for as long as it takes to keep the voices of the past at bay so that your husband can make the decision to not listen to them.

Prayer

Lord, I pray that You would enable (husband's name) to let go of his past completely. Deliver him from any hold it has on him. Help him to put off his former conduct and habitual ways of thinking about it and be renewed in his mind

(Ephesians 4:22,23). Enlarge his understanding to know that You make all things new (Revelation 21:5). Show him a fresh, Holy Spirit-inspired way of relating to negative things that have happened. Give him the mind of Christ so that he can clearly discern Your voice from the voices of the past. When he hears those old voices, enable him to rise up and shut them down with the truth of Your Word. Where he has formerly experienced rejection or pain, I pray he not allow them to color what he sees and hears now. Pour forgiveness into his heart so that bitterness, resentment, revenge, and unforgiveness will have no place there. May he regard the past as only a history lesson and not a guide for his daily life. Wherever his past has become an unpleasant memory, I pray You would redeem it and bring life out of it. Bind up his wounds (Psalm 147:3). Restore his soul (Psalm 23:3). Help him to release the past so that he will not live in it, but learn from it, break out of it, and move into the future You have for him.

POWER TOOLS

Do not remember the former things, nor consider the things of old. Behold, I will do a new thing, now it shall spring forth; shall you not know it? I will even make a road in the wilderness and rivers in the desert.

ISAIAH 43:18,19

If anyone is in Christ, he is a new creation; old things have passed away; behold, all things have become new.

2 CORINTHIANS 5:17

Put off, concerning your former conduct, the
old man which grows corrupt according to the
deceitful lusts, and be renewed in the spirit of
your mind, and . . . put on the new man
which was created according to God,
in true righteousness and holiness.
EPHESIANS 4:22-24

Even though our outward man is perishing, yet the
inward man is being renewed day by day.
2 CORINTHIANS 4:16

God will wipe away every tear from their eyes;
there shall be no more death, nor sorrow, nor crying;
and there shall be no more pain, for the former
things have passed away.
REVELATION 21:4

CHAPTER TWENTY

His Attitude

N o one wants to be around a person with a bad attitude. Life is hard enough without listening to someone constantly complaining in your ear. I know a man who is so in the habit of being angry and miserable that it is his first reaction to everything— even good news. When great things happen, he finds something to be upset about. Unfortunately, this was modeled to him as a child, so it was probably a learned response. Perhaps no one ever showed him how to enjoy life. But allowing the past to control today is still a choice he makes. Because of that, not only will he never be happy, but neither will those around him. We don't want to be that kind of person, nor do we want to live with one.

Without naming names, let me assure you that I am an expert when it comes to praying for someone with a bad attitude. It took me a long time, however, to stop reacting to the negativity and start praying about it instead. It has paid off, but I'm still perfecting this mode of operation. Every time I prayed for a spirit of joy to arise in this person's heart, I saw visible changes and my reaction was better as well.

An angry, dour, unforgiving, negative person can get that way for various reasons. He *stays* that way because of a stubborn will that refuses to receive God's love. The Bible says we have a choice as to what we will allow into our heart (Psalm 101:4), and whether we will harden it to the love of God or not (Proverbs 28:14). We choose our attitude. We choose to receive the love of the Lord. We permit an attitude of thankfulness to rise in us.

If your husband allows himself to wallow in a consistently bad attitude, it will make a good marriage miserable, and a shaky marriage intolerable. A habit of responding negatively will adversely affect every aspect of his life. Of course you can't rule over your husband's will, but you can pray that his will lines up with God's. Pray that his heart becomes pure, because the Bible promises a person who has a pure heart will see God (Matthew 5:8) and have a cheerful countenance (Proverbs 15:13). (Who doesn't wish her husband could see God and have a cheerful countenance?) Pray for his heart to be filled with praise, thanksgiving, love, and joy, because "a good man out of the good treasure of his heart brings forth good things" (Matthew 12:35). Even if there are no major changes immediately, he is certain to be softened by your prayers. And that, at least, can give *you* a better attitude while you wait for his to improve.

Prayer

Lord, fill (husband's name) with Your love and peace today. May there be a calmness, serenity, and sense of well-being established in him because his life is God-controlled, rather than flesh-controlled. Enable him to walk in his house with a clean and perfect heart before You (Psalm 101:2). Shine the light of Your Spirit upon him and fill him with Your love.

I pray that he will be kind and patient, not selfish or easily provoked. Enable him to bear all things, believe all things, hope all things, and endure all things (1 Corinthians 13:7). Release him from anger, unrest, anxiety, concerns, inner turmoil, strife, and pressure. May he not be broken in spirit because of sorrow (Proverbs 15:13), but enjoy the continual feast of a merry heart (Proverbs 15:15). Give him a spirit of joy and keep him from growing into a grumpy old man. Help him to be anxious for nothing, but give thanks in all things so he can know the peace that passes all understanding. May he come to the point of saying, "I have learned in whatever state I am, to be content" (Philippians 4:11). I say to (husband's name) this day, "The LORD bless you and keep you; the LORD make His face shine upon you, and be gracious to you; the LORD lift up His countenance upon you, and give you peace" (Numbers 6:24-26).

POWER TOOLS

Be anxious for nothing, but in everything by prayer
and supplication, with thanksgiving, let your requests
be made known to God; and the peace of God,
which surpasses all understanding, will guard your
hearts and minds through Christ Jesus.
PHILIPPIANS 4:6,7

Cast away from you all the transgressions which
you have committed, and get yourselves a
new heart and a new spirit.
EZEKIEL 18:31

Whoever has no rule over his own spirit is
like a city broken down, without walls.
PROVERBS 25:28

Though I have the gift of prophecy, and understand
all mysteries and all knowledge, and though I have
all faith, so that I could remove mountains,
but have not love, I am nothing.
1 CORINTHIANS 13:2

Enter into His gates with thanksgiving,
and into His courts with praise.
Be thankful to Him, and bless His name.
PSALM 100:4

CHAPTER TWENTY-ONE

His Marriage

efore I was married, one of the traits I knew I wanted in a husband was an avid disinterest in sports. I detested the thought of being with someone the rest of my life who spent every spare moment on a couch with remote in hand, watching football, baseball, basketball, and golf. One of the things I admired most about Michael when we first started dating was that he never mentioned sports when we were together. In fact, he claimed to be completely bored with them. You can imagine how shocked I was when, several years after we were married, he became not merely interested in sports, but obsessed. If the Chicago Bears lost, so, ultimately, did the rest of the family. When the Cubs won, everyone around him went deaf from his screaming. He wasn't content to see an occasional game; he had to see *every* game. He wasn't a passive observer. He dressed up in Bear T-shirts and Cub hats and jumped up and down. I tried going to games with him, but I found more intrigue in the hot dogs. I tried watching sports with him on TV, but the boredom was excruciating. I gave in to resentment over the fact that it seemed he would rather watch a sporting event than spend time with his family.

It wasn't until years later, when I really started praying about our marriage, that things changed. For some reason unfathomable to me, God didn't take away my husband's interest in sports like I prayed. Instead, He gave me peace and a new perspective on it. We worked out a compromise where I wouldn't pressure him to deny himself sports, if he wouldn't put pressure on me to feign interest. I would not accuse him of tactical deception before we were married, if he would allow me the same courtesy. This may seem like a minor concern in a marriage, but these kinds of things add up and can become pivotal in determining whether a marriage stays together or falls apart.

Praying about all aspects of a marriage keeps the concept of divorce from gaining any hold. So we mustn't neglect the major issues, even if we think they don't apply to us. From the day we were married, I prayed that there would be no divorce or adultery in our future. Although there was no history of either of those in our family backgrounds, divorce and adultery had so saturated our culture and the business we were in that they were almost expected in some circles. I prayed that God would preserve our marriage from any such destruction. He has been faithful to answer those prayers.

Marriage is great when two people enter into it with a mutual commitment to keep it strong no matter what. But often a couple will have preconceived ideas about who the other is and how married life is supposed to be, and then reality hits. That's when their kingdom can become divided. You have to continually pray that any unreal expectations be exposed and all incompatibilities be smoothed out so that you grow together in a spirit of unity, commitment, and a bond of intimacy. Pray that your marriage is a place where two agree so God will be in the midst of it (Matthew 18:19,20). If either of you has been married before, pray that you do not bring any residue from that into your marriage now. Break any ties—good or bad, emotional or spiritual—with any former relationships. You can't move forward into the future if you have a foot stuck in the past.

Don't take your marriage for granted, no matter how great it is. "Let him who thinks he stands take heed lest he fall" (1 Corinthians 10:12). Pray for your marriage to be protected from any person or situation that could destroy it. Ask the Lord to do whatever it takes to keep the marriage intact, even if it means striking one of you with lightning when you think about giving it all up! Pray that God will make your marriage a source of joy and life to both of you, and not a drudgery, a thorn, a dread, an irritation, or a temporary condition.

Prayer

Lord, I pray You would protect our marriage from anything that would harm or destroy it. Shield it from our own selfishness and neglect, from the evil plans and desires of others, and from unhealthy or dangerous situations. May there be no thoughts of divorce or infidelity in our hearts, and none in our future. Set us free from past hurts, memories, and ties from previous relationships, and unrealistic expectations of one another. I pray that there be no jealousy in either of us, or the low self-esteem that precedes that. Let nothing come into our hearts and habits that would threaten the marriage in any way, especially influences like alcohol, drugs, gambling, pornography, lust, or obsessions.

Unite us in a bond of friendship, commitment, generosity, and understanding. Eliminate our immaturity, hostility, or feelings of inadequacy. Help us to make time for one another alone, to nurture and renew the marriage and remind ourselves of the reasons we were married in the first place. I pray that (husband's name) will be so committed to You, Lord, that his commitment to me will not waiver, no matter what storms come. I pray that our love for each other will grow stronger every day, so that we will never leave a legacy of divorce to our children.

POWER TOOLS

Two are better than one, because they have a good reward for their labor. For if they fall, one will lift up his companion. But woe to him who is alone when he falls, for he has no one to help him up.
ECCLESIASTES 4:9,10

Take heed to your spirit, and let none deal treacherously with the wife of his youth. For the LORD God of Israel says that He hates divorce, "for it covers one's garment with violence," says the LORD of hosts. Therefore take heed to your spirit, that you do not deal treacherously.
MALACHI 2:15,16

Marriage is honorable among all, and the bed undefiled; but fornicators and adulterers God will judge.
HEBREWS 13:4

If two lie down together, they will keep warm;
but how can one be warm alone?
ECCLESIASTES 4:11

Now to the married I command, yet not I but the
Lord: A wife is not to depart from her husband. But
even if she does depart, let her remain unmarried or
be reconciled to her husband. And a husband is not
to divorce his wife.
1 CORINTHIANS 7:10,11

CHAPTER TWENTY-TWO

His Emotions

*D*on used anger to control his family. Each family member was so concerned about his temper that they lived their lives on tiptoe, doing his bidding out of fear rather than love. When his wife, Jenny, learned she not only didn't have to tolerate his anger, but going along with it was disobedient to God, things began to change: "Make no friendship with an angry man, and with a furious man do not go, lest you learn his ways and set a snare for your soul" (Proverbs 22:24,25).

Jenny realized she could still love the man but not approve of his sin, so she began praying fervently for him on a regular basis, both alone and with a group of prayer partners. She prayed he would stop being controlled by his emotions, and instead be controlled by the Holy Spirit. Her prayers not only helped to clear his mind enough for him to see how he had been acting, but they paved the way for him to find strength and courage to alter his behavior. "A gift in secret pacifies anger" (Proverbs 21:14). The best gift a wife can give in secret to calm her husband's anger is to pray for him.

Chad was tormented for years by chronic depression. Although his wife, Marilyn, was an upbeat person, his negative emotions brought her down and made her feel hopeless and depressed just like he was. Then she read about King David's experiences and recognized they described exactly what her husband had been feeling. "My soul is full of troubles, and my life draws near to the grave. I am counted with those who go down to the pit; I am like a man who has no strength" (Psalm 88:3,4). "I am troubled, I am bowed down greatly; I go mourning all the day long". . . . "I am feeble and severely broken; I groan because of the turmoil of my heart" (Psalm 38:6,8).

Marilyn saw that in spite of such deep despair, David found his hope in the Lord and rose above it. "O LORD, You have brought my soul up from the grave; You have kept me alive, that I should not go down to the pit" (Psalm 30:3). "I will be glad and rejoice in Your mercy, for You have considered my trouble; You have known my soul in adversities" (Psalm 31:7). "Draw near to my soul, and redeem it" (Psalm 69:18). She felt God surely had compassion for Chad and it sparked hope in her that prayer was the key to his freedom from the grips of depression.

She told Chad she had committed to pray for him every day and wanted him to keep her informed as to how he was feeling. From the first day, they both noticed that every time she prayed, his spirit lifted. Soon he could no longer deny the power of prayer and he began to pray along with her. He has been steadily improving ever since. His depressions are less frequent now and he is able to rise above them far more quickly. The two of them are committed to seek God for Chad's total freedom.

Anger and depression are but two of the many negative emotions that can torment a man's soul. Often they are only an habitual way of thinking that has been given place over time. Men tend to believe it's part of their character that can't be altered, but these patterns can be broken. Don't stand by and watch your husband be manipulated by his emotions. Freedom may be just a prayer away.

Prayer

Lord, You have said in Your Word that You redeem our souls when we put our trust in You (Psalm 34:22). I pray that (husband's name) would have faith in You to redeem his soul from negative emotions. May he never be controlled by depression, anger, anxiety, jealousy, hopelessness, fear, or suicidal thoughts. Specifically I pray about (area of concern). Deliver him from this and all other controlling emotions (Psalm 40:17). I know that only You can deliver and heal, but use me as Your instrument of restoration. Help me not to be pulled down with him when he struggles. Enable me instead to understand and have words to say that will bring life.

Free him to share his deepest feelings with me and others who can help. Liberate him to cry when he needs to and not bottle his emotions inside. At the same time, give him the gift of laughter and ability to find humor in even serious situations. Teach him to take his eyes off his circumstances and trust in You, regardless of how he is feeling. Give him patience to possess his soul and the ability to take charge of it (Luke 21:19). Anoint him with "the oil of joy" (Isaiah 61:3), refresh him with Your Spirit, and set him free from negative emotions this day.

POWER TOOLS

He who trusts in his own heart is a fool, but
whoever walks wisely will be delivered.
PROVERBS 28:26

The eye of the LORD is on those who fear Him,
on those who hope in His mercy, to deliver
their soul from death.
PSALM 33:18,19

I waited patiently for the LORD; and He inclined to
me, and heard my cry. He also brought me up out of
a horrible pit, out of the miry clay, and set my feet
upon a rock, and established my steps. He has put a
new song in my mouth—praise to our God; many
will see it and fear, and will trust in the LORD.
PSALM 40:1-3

He restores my soul; He leads me in the paths of
righteousness for His name's sake.
PSALM 23:3

The LORD redeems the soul of His servants, and none
of those who trust in Him shall be condemned.
PSALM 34:22

CHAPTER TWENTY-THREE

His Walk

A man's walk is the way he journeys through life—his direction, his focus, the steps he takes. Every day he chooses a path. One path will take him forward. All others will take him back. The way he walks affects every aspect of his being—how he relates to other people, how he treats his family, how people view him, even how he looks. I've seen men who were unattractive by any standard change radically as they learned to walk with the Spirit of God. As His image became imprinted upon theirs, they developed a richness of soul, a glorious purity, and an inner confidence of knowing what direction they were going. This gave them a strength and a sense of purpose that is not only attractive and appealing, it's magnetic.

The Bible reveals much about the kind of walk we should have. We are to walk with *moral correctness* because "no good thing will He withhold from those who walk uprightly" (Psalm 84:11). We are to walk *without fault* because "whoever walks blamelessly will be saved" (Proverbs 28:18). We are to walk with *godly advisors* because "blessed

is the man who walks not in the counsel of the ungodly"
(Psalm 1:1). We are to walk in *obedience* because "blessed
is every one who fears the LORD, who walks in His ways"
(Psalm 128:1). We are to walk with *people of wisdom* because "he who walks with wise men will be wise" (Proverbs
13:20). We are to walk with *integrity* because "he who
walks with integrity walks securely" (Proverbs 10:9). Most
of all, we are to walk a path of holiness. "A highway shall
be there, and a road, and it shall be called the Highway of
Holiness. The unclean shall not pass over it, but it shall be
for others. Whoever walks the road, although a fool, shall
not go astray" (Isaiah 35:8). The best part about walking
on the Highway of Holiness is that even if we end up
doing something dumb, we still won't get thrown off
the path.

Debra's husband, Ben, is a godly man who would not be
considered a foolish person. However, he did make an im-
pulsive investment of a rather large sum of money which, in
hindsight, proved to be a very foolish move. All that money
was lost, and more, because there were added expenses as a
result. This matter could have destroyed their finances and
possibly even their health and their marriage, but because
Ben had a solid walk of obedience and holiness before the
Lord, they were spared. The fact that he ran ahead on the
path and foolishly didn't wait for God's direction got him
into trouble, but not to his destruction.

Jesus said there is only one way to get on the right path,
one door through which to enter. "I am the way," He says
(John 14:6). The way that leads to destruction is wide and
broad and many choose to go that route. But "narrow is the
gate and difficult is the way which leads to life, and there
are few who find it" (Matthew 7:14). Pray for your husband
to find it. Pray that he is guided by God's Holy Spirit. Pray

that he stays on the path by having faith in God's Word, a heart for obedience, and deep repentance for any actions he takes that are not God's will for his life. Faith and obedience will get him on the Highway of Holiness; walking in the Spirit, and not in the flesh, will keep him there.

God desires that your husband's every step be led by Him (Galatians 5:25), so He can walk with him and grow him into His image. A man who walks with God is very desirable indeed.

Prayer

"*O Lord*, I know the way of man is not in himself; it is not in man who walks to direct his own steps" (Jeremiah 10:23). Therefore, Lord, I pray that *You* would direct my husband's steps. Lead him in *Your* light, teach him *Your* way, so he will walk in *Your* truth. I pray that he would have a deeper walk with You and an ever progressing hunger for *Your* Word. May Your presence be like a delicacy he never ceases to crave. Lead him on Your path and make him quick to confess when he strays from it. Reveal to him any hidden sin that would hinder him from walking rightly before You. May he experience deep repentance when he doesn't live in obedience to Your laws. Create in him a clean heart and renew a steadfast spirit within him. Don't cast him away from Your presence, and do not take Your Holy Spirit from him (Psalm 51:10,11).

Lord, Your Word says that those who are in the flesh cannot please You (Romans 8:8). So I pray that You will enable (husband's name) to walk in the Spirit and not in the flesh and thereby keep himself "from the paths of the destroyer" (Psalm 17:4). As he walks in the Spirit, may he bear the fruit of the Spirit, which is love, joy, peace, patience, kindness, goodness, faithfulness, gentleness, and self-control (Galatians 5:22,23). Keep him on the Highway of Holiness so that the way he walks will be integrated into every part of his life.

POWER TOOLS

Walk worthy of the calling with which you were called, with all lowliness and gentleness, with long-suffering, bearing with one another in love.
EPHESIANS 4:1,2

He who walks righteously and speaks uprightly, he who despises the gain of oppressions, who gestures with his hands, refusing bribes, who stops his ears from hearing of bloodshed, and shuts his eyes from seeing evil: he will dwell on high; his place of defense will be the fortress of rocks; bread will be given him, his water will be sure.
ISAIAH 33:15,16

Having these promises, beloved, let us cleanse ourselves from all filthiness of the flesh and spirit, perfecting holiness in the fear of God.
2 CORINTHIANS 7:1

LORD, who may abide in Your tabernacle? Who may dwell in Your holy hill? He who walks uprightly, and works righteousness, and speaks the truth in his heart.
PSALM 15:1,2

My eyes shall be on the faithful of the land,
that they may dwell with me; he who walks in
a perfect way, he shall serve me.
PSALM 101:6

CHAPTER TWENTY-FOUR

His Talk

*H*ave you ever observed a man who is all talk and no action? There are some men who spend more time bragging about what they are going to do than actually doing it. They typically never get anywhere. "A dream comes through much activity, and a fool's voice is known by his many words" (Ecclesiastes 5:3). Dreams don't come true when more time is spent talking about them than praying and working toward achieving them.

Have you been around a man who is angry, crass, or ungodly in his speech? His bad language gives his listeners a sick, uncomfortable feeling and they don't want to be around him. "Let all bitterness, wrath, anger, clamor, and evil speaking be put away from you, with all malice" (Ephesians 4:31). The good things of life seem to overlook those who have nothing good coming out of their mouths.

Have you known a man who complains all the time? No matter what's happening, he finds something negative to grumble about. "Do all things without murmuring and disputing, that you may become blameless and harmless, children of God without fault in the midst of a crooked and perverse generation, among whom you shine as lights in the world" (Philippians 2:14,15). Negative words bring negative results and things seldom turn out right for a person who continually uses them.

Are you acquainted with a man who is quick to speak yet does not seriously consider what he is saying? He blurts out words without weighing the effect of them. "The heart of the righteous studies how to answer, but the mouth of the wicked pours forth evil" (Proverbs 15:28). "Do you see a man hasty in his words? There is more hope for a fool than for him" (Proverbs 29:20). Much grief is in the future of anyone who doesn't consider the consequences of his spoken words.

Have you seen a man speak discouragement and pain into someone—a spouse, a child, a friend, a coworker? "Death and life are in the power of the tongue, and those who love it will eat its fruit" (Proverbs 18:21). That man will bring *destruction* into his own life because of it.

Our words can justify us or condemn us (Matthew 12:37). They can bring us joy (Proverbs 15:23), or corrupt and dishonor us (Matthew 15:11). What we say can either build up or break down the soul of whomever we are speaking to (Proverbs 15:4). The consequences of what we speak are so great that our words can lead us to ruin or save our lives (Proverbs 13:3).

Everyone has a choice about what he or she says, and there are rewards for making the right one. "Whoever guards his mouth and tongue keeps his soul from troubles" (Proverbs 21:23). Listen to the way your husband talks. What comes out of his mouth has to do with the condition of his heart. "For out of the abundance of the heart the mouth speaks" (Matthew 12:34). If you hear him complaining, speaking negatively, talking like a fool, or speaking words that bring destruction and death into his or anyone else's life, he is suffering from negative heart overflow. Pray for the Holy Spirit to convict his heart, fill it with His love, peace, and joy, and teach him a new way to talk.

Prayer

Lord, I pray Your Holy Spirit would guard my husband's mouth so that he will speak only words that edify and bring life. Help him to not be a grumbler, complainer, a user of foul language, or one who destroys with his words, but be disciplined enough to keep his conversation godly. Your Word says a man who desires a long life must keep his tongue from evil and his lips from speaking deceit (Psalm 34:12-13). Show him how to do that. Fill him with Your love so that out of the overflow of his heart will come words that build up and not tear down. Work that in my heart as well.

May Your Spirit of love reign in the words we speak so that we don't miscommunicate or wound one another. Help us to show each other respect, speak words that encourage, share our feelings openly, and come to mutual agreements without strife. Lord, You've said in Your Word that when two agree, You are in their midst. I pray that the reverse be true as well—that You will be in our midst so that we two can agree. Let the words of our mouths and the meditations of our hearts be acceptable in Your sight, O Lord, our strength and our Redeemer (Psalm 19:14).

POWER TOOLS

Let no corrupt word proceed out of your mouth, but
what is good for necessary edification, that it may im-
part grace to the hearers.
EPHESIANS 4:29

For every idle word men may speak, they will give
account of it in the day of judgment.
MATTHEW 12:36

Who is the man who desires life, and loves many
days, that he may see good? Keep your tongue from
evil, and your lips from speaking deceit.
PSALM 34:12,13

The words of a wise man's mouth are gracious, but
the lips of a fool shall swallow him up.
ECCLESIASTES 10:12

Those things which proceed out of the mouth come
from the heart, and they defile a man.
MATTHEW 15:18

CHAPTER TWENTY-FIVE

His Repentance

*S*uzanne prayed every day for years that her husband, Jerry, would stop using drugs. Over and over she caught him doing the same thing. Each time he would confess it, say he was sorry, and swear he wasn't going to do it again. But time and again he fell. She never gave up praying for true repentance to happen in his heart—the kind that turns a man around to walk in a different direction. Unfortunately, Jerry had to learn some hard and painful lessons before God got his attention, but eventually there was a life-changing transformation. Today he is a new man, and together with Suzanne he has a public ministry helping people with similar problems. Suzanne was a praying wife who never stopped believing that God would bring her husband to repentance.

Everyone makes mistakes. That's not the issue. But there is an epidemic in the world today of people who can't admit they did something wrong. God says, "If we confess our sins, He is faithful and just to forgive us our sins and to cleanse us from all unrighteousness" (1 John 1:9). But first we have to be sorry about what we've done.

According to God's way of doing things, there are three steps to changing our behavior. First there is *confession*, which is *admitting* what we did. Next there is *repentance*, which is *being sorry* about what we did. Then there is *asking forgiveness*, which is *being cleansed and released* from what we did. The inability or resistance to do any of these three steps is rooted in pride. A man who can't humble himself to admit he's wrong before God and before man will have problems in his life that never go away. "Do you see a man wise in his own eyes? There is more hope for a fool than for him" (Proverbs 26:12).

Does your husband have trouble confessing his faults? Or is he the kind of person who can say "I'm sorry" twenty times a day, yet the behavior he apologizes for never changes? In either case, he needs a repentant heart. True repentance means having so much remorse over what you've done that you don't do it again. Only God can cause us to see our sin for what it is, and feel about it the same way He does. "The goodness of God leads you to repentance" (Romans 2:4). Repentance is a working of God's grace, and we can pray for it to be worked in our husbands.

Too many men have fallen because of pride and the inability to confess and repent. We see it all the time. We read about it in the newspapers. Unconfessed sin doesn't just go away. It becomes a cancer that grows and suffocates life. Pray for your husband to be convicted of his sin, to humbly confess it before God, then turn from his error and cease to do it. God is "not willing that any should perish but that all should come to repentance" (2 Peter 3:9). This kind of prayer can be very annoying to the one being prayed for, but it's far easier to have God shine His light upon our sin than it is to experience the consequences of it. Your husband will be thankful in the end, even if he won't admit it.

Prayer

Lord, I pray that You would convict my husband of any error in his life. Let there be "nothing covered that will not be revealed, and hidden that will not be known" (Matthew 10:26). Cleanse him from any secret sins and teach him to be a person who is quick to confess when he is wrong (Psalm 19:12). Help him to recognize his mistakes. Give him eyes to see Your truth and ears to hear Your voice. Bring him to full repentance before You. If there is suffering to be done, let it be the suffering of a remorseful heart and not because the crushing hand of the enemy has found an opening into his life through unconfessed sin. Lord, I know that humility must come before honor (Proverbs 15:33). Take away all pride that would cause him to deny his faults and work into his soul a humility of heart so that he will receive the honor You have for him.

POWER TOOLS

If our heart does not condemn us, we have confidence toward God. And whatever we ask we receive from Him, because we keep His commandments and do those things that are pleasing in His sight.
1 JOHN 3:21,22

He who covers his sins will not prosper, but whoever confesses and forsakes them will have mercy.
PROVERBS 28:13

Search me, O God, and know my heart; try me, and know my anxieties; and see if there is any wicked way in me, and lead me in the way everlasting.
PSALM 139:23,24

When I kept silent, my bones grew old through my
groaning all the day long. For day and night Your
hand was heavy upon me; my vitality was turned into
the drought of summer. I acknowledged my sin to
You, and my iniquity I have not hidden. I said, "I will
confess my transgressions to the LORD," and You forgave the iniquity of my sin.

PSALM 32:3-5

A servant of the Lord must not quarrel but be gentle
to all, able to teach, patient, in humility correcting
those who are in opposition, if God perhaps will
grant them repentance, so that they may know the
truth, and that they may come to their senses and
escape the snare of the devil, having been taken
captive by him to do his will.

2 TIMOTHY 2:24-26

CHAPTER TWENTY-SIX

His Deliverance

*M*elissa was concerned about her husband's attraction to alcohol. Mark wasn't exactly an alcoholic, but he was exhibiting symptoms reminiscent of his father, who *was* an alcoholic. She prayed for a breaking of any similar tendency that may have been passed on to her husband, and she also prayed that their children would not inherit the weakness either. She asked God to protect them all from even the *symptoms* of alcoholism. To this day her husband has not become an alcoholic and her teenagers show no signs of it. She feels the power of God in answer to her prayers has played a major part in keeping them from inheriting this condition.

Stephanie had been married to Jason only a short time before she realized he struggled with a spirit of lust. It wasn't that he didn't love her. He was dealing with the sins of his past—a promiscuous lifestyle from which he had never thoroughly distanced himself or renounced. Once she recognized it as something he was captive to, she prayed for his deliverance. Because he wanted that, too, it wasn't long before he was set free from it.

Everyone needs deliverance at certain times, because there are all kinds of things that can pull us into bondage. God knows this. Why would Jesus have come as the Deliverer if we didn't need one? Why would He have instructed us to pray, "Deliver us from the evil one" (Matthew 6:13) if we didn't need to be? Why does He promise to deliver us from temptation (2 Peter 2:9), the clutches of dangerous people (Psalm 140:1), our self-destructive tendencies (Proverbs 24:11), *all* of our troubles (Psalm 34:17), and death (2 Corinthians 1:10), if He doesn't intend to do it? He is ready and willing. We just have to ask. "Call upon Me in the day of trouble; I will deliver you, and you shall glorify Me" (Psalm 50:15).

Isn't it comforting to know that when we feel imprisoned by the death grip of our circumstances, God hears our cries for freedom? He sees our need. "He looked down from the height of His sanctuary; from heaven the LORD viewed the earth, to hear the groaning of the prisoner, to release those appointed to death" (Psalm 102:19,20). How glorious to embrace the certainty that when there seems to be no way out, God can miraculously lift us up and away from whatever is seeking to devour us (Psalm 25:15). Who doesn't need that?

Even if your husband finds it difficult to admit he needs help—some men feel like failures if they can't do it all themselves—your prayers can still be instrumental in his finding deliverance. You can pray to the Deliverer to set him free from anything that binds him. You can stand strong, through your prayers, against the enemy who seeks to put him into bondage. "Stand fast therefore in the liberty by which Christ has made us free, and do not be entangled again with a yoke of bondage" (Galatians 5:1). The best way I know to stand strong is to put on the whole armor of

God. That's the way I pray for myself and my husband and I have found it to be most effective. Rather than explain it, let me show you how to pray it.

Prayer

Lord, You have said to call upon You in the day of trouble and You will deliver us (Psalm 50:15). I call upon You now and ask that You would work deliverance in my husband's life. Deliver him from anything that binds him. Set him free from (name a specific thing). Deliver him quickly and be a rock of refuge and a fortress of defense to save him (Psalm 31:2). Lift him away from the hands of the enemy (Psalm 31:15).

Bring him to a place of understanding where he can recognize the work of evil and cry out to You for help. If the deliverance he prays for isn't immediate, keep him from discouragement and help him to be confident that You have begun a good work in him and will complete it (Philippians 1:6). Give him the certainty that even in his most hopeless state, when he finds it impossible to change anything, You, Lord, can change everything.

Help him understand that "we do not wrestle against flesh and blood, but against principalities, against powers, against the rulers of the darkness of this age, against spiritual hosts of wickedness in the heavenly places" (Ephesians 6:12). I pray that he will be strong in the Lord and put on the whole armor of God, so he can stand against the wiles of the devil in the evil day. Help him to gird his waist with truth and put on the breastplate of righteousness, having shod his feet with the preparation of the gospel of peace. Enable him to take up the shield of faith, with which to quench all the fiery darts of the wicked one. I pray that he will take the helmet of salvation, and the sword of the Spirit, which is the Word of God, praying always with all prayer and supplication in the Spirit, being watchful and standing strong to the end (Ephesians 6:13-18).

POWER TOOLS

The LORD is my rock and my fortress and my deliverer; my God, my strength, in whom I will trust; my shield and the horn of my salvation, my stronghold. I will call upon the LORD, who is worthy to be praised; so shall I be saved from my enemies.
PSALM 18:2,3

Because he has set his love upon Me, therefore I will deliver him; I will set him on high, because he has known My name.
PSALM 91:14

He sent from above, He took me; He drew me out of many waters. He delivered me from my strong enemy, from those who hated me, for they were too strong for me. They confronted me in the day of my calamity, but the LORD was my support. He also brought me out into a broad place; He delivered me because He delighted in me.
PSALM 18:16-19

You have delivered my soul from death. Have You
not delivered my feet from falling, that I may walk
before God in the light of the living?
PSALM 56:13

The Spirit of the LORD is upon Me, because He has
anointed Me to preach the gospel to the poor; He
has sent Me to heal the brokenhearted, to proclaim
liberty to the captives and recovery of sight to the
blind, to set at liberty those who are oppressed.
LUKE 4:18

CHAPTER TWENTY-SEVEN

His Obedience

*L*isa was concerned that her husband, Jonathan, was not growing spiritually the way she was. Her relationship with the Lord was deepening every day while his appeared to be shrinking just as rapidly. She was frustrated with his lack of spiritual commitment, because she longed for them to grow together and have a shared experience in this vital area of their lives. She didn't want to be the spiritual heavyweight in the family. Whenever she said anything about it, Jonathan protested, saying his career kept him too busy to spend time with the Lord and read His Word. Even his business trips often took him out of town on weekends so he missed attending church with Lisa and their children.

The thing that bothered *her* most was that none of this seemed to bother *him*—that is until his work became more challenging than he could comfortably handle. As he grew increasingly stressed, Lisa could see how depleting it was for him. She knew that if he could make the connection between spending time with the Lord every day and finding spiritual strength, his life would be far better. She also was certain he wasn't ready to hear about it from her.

Even though Lisa knew that God was calling Jonathan to this step of obedience, she determined not to say anything. Instead she prayed every day for him to have the desire for more of God in his life. Although she prayed for months without any visible change, one morning he quietly announced, "I'm going to the office earlier today because I need time alone with the Lord before I do anything else."

She silently thanked God.

Since then, with only a few exceptions, he has left home early every week-day morning to read his Bible and pray in his office. That was two years ago and now this spiritual discipline has carried over into areas of physical discipline as well. He is exercising, eating right, losing the weight he wanted to lose, and gaining new stamina. Only God can do that.

If you clearly observe your husband walking down a wrong path, should you say something? If so, how much should you say and when is the right time to say it? The best way I've found to proceed is to take it to God *first* and weigh it on *His* scales. He may instruct you to just be quiet and pray, like He did with Lisa. But if He does direct you to speak to your husband about the matter, there will be a far greater chance of him hearing God's voice somewhere in your words if you've prayed *before* you speak. Anything perceived as nagging will be counterproductive and better left unsaid. Praying that his eyes be opened to the truth and his heart convicted will be far more effective than you telling him what to do. You can *encourage* him to do what's right and *pray* for him to do what's right, but ultimately it's God's voice that will have the greatest impact.

No man can receive all God has for him if he is not living in obedience. Jesus, who was never one to beat around the bush, said, "If you want to enter into life, keep the commandments" (Matthew 19:17). He knew that nothing would give a man more peace and confidence than knowing he is doing what God wants him to do. God's Word promises that by being obedient to His ways your husband will find mercy (Psalm 25:10), peace (Psalm 37:37), happiness (Proverbs 29:18), plenty (Proverbs 21:5), blessings (Luke 11:28), and life (Proverbs 21:21). *Not* living in obedience brings harsh consequences (Proverbs 15:10), unanswered prayers (Proverbs 28:9), and the inability to enter into the great things God has for him (1 Corinthians 6:9).

Walking in obedience has to do not only with keeping God's commandments, but also with heeding God's *specific* instructions. For example, if God has instructed your husband to rest and he doesn't do it, that's disobedience. If He has told him to stop doing a certain type of work and he keeps doing it, that's disobedience. If He has told him to move to another place and he doesn't move, that's disobedience, too.

A man who does what God asks, builds his house on a rock. When the rain, floods, and wind come and beat on the house, it won't fall (Matthew 7:24-27). You don't want to witness the downfall of your house because of your husband's disobedience in any area. While it's not your place to be either his mother or the gestapo, it is your job to pray, and speak *after* you've gotten your orders from God.

If your husband's disobedience to God's ways has already brought down your house in some manner, know that God will honor *your* obedience and He will see that you will not be destroyed. He will pour His blessings on you and restore what has been lost. Just keep praying that your husband not have a hearing problem when it comes to the voice of God, and that he has the strength, courage, and motivation to act on what he hears.

Prayer

Lord, You have said in Your Word that if we regard iniquity in our hearts, You will not hear (Psalm 66:18). I want You to hear my prayers, so I ask You to reveal where there is any disobedience in my life, especially with regard to my husband. Show me if I'm selfish, unloving, critical, angry, resentful, unforgiving, or bitter toward him. Show me where I have not obeyed You or lived Your way. I confess it as sin and ask for Your forgiveness.

I pray that You would give (husband's name) a desire to live in obedience to Your laws and Your ways. Reveal and uproot anything he willingly gives place to that is not of You. Help him to bring every thought and action under Your control. Remind him to do good, speak evil of no one, and be peaceable, gentle, and humble (Titus 3:1,2). Teach him to embrace the stretching pain of discipline and discipleship. Reward him according to his righteousness and according to the cleanness of his hands (Psalm 18:20). Show him Your ways, O Lord; teach him Your paths. Lead him in Your truth, for You are the God of his salvation (Psalm 25:4,5).

Make him a praising person, for I know that when we worship You we gain clear understanding, our lives are transformed, and we receive power to live Your way. Help him to hear Your specific instructions to him and enable him to obey them. Give him a heart that longs to do Your will and may he enjoy the peace that can only come from living in total obedience to Your commands.

POWER TOOLS

My son, do not forget my law, but let your heart
keep my commands; for length of days and long life
and peace they will add to you. Let not mercy and
truth forsake you; bind them around your neck, write
them on the tablet of your heart.
PROVERBS 3:1-3

Not everyone who says to Me, "Lord, Lord," shall
enter the kingdom of heaven, but he who does the
will of My Father in heaven.
MATTHEW 7:21

One who turns away his ear from hearing the law,
even his prayer shall be an abomination.
PROVERBS 28:9

Obey My voice, and I will be your God, and you
shall be My people. And walk in all the ways that I
have commanded you, that it may be well with you.
JEREMIAH 7:23

CHAPTER TWENTY-EIGHT

His Self-Image

*W*hy do some very capable and talented men consistently find doors of opportunity and acceptance closed to them, while others with equal or less ability have seemingly unlimited opportunities and success in every area of their lives? It doesn't seem fair. Timing, of course, has something to do with it. God has a time for everything and He works in us what needs to be done to prepare us for what is ahead. Having a sense of God's timing brings the peace to wait on the Lord for it.

There can be another important reason for the struggle, however, and that is a man's perception of himself. If he has a poor self-image, he will have doubts about his value that creep into everything he does—even into his relationships. People who are uncomfortable with his insecurity may avoid him, and this will in turn affect how he relates to his family, friends, coworkers, and even strangers. Expecting to be rejected, he will be.

Dan experienced great frustration trying to find his way in life. He didn't know who he was or where he fit in, or if in fact he fit in anywhere. His preoccupation with trying to figure it all out caused great friction between him and his wife, Cindy. She tried to help him, but he resented her advice. He perceived her thoughts and suggestions as mocking his ability to figure things out for himself. His reaction was to dismiss her words, which caused her to strive even more to assert herself. The harder Cindy fought to not feel devalued, the more Dan retaliated, until in the frustration of his own insecurity he rejected her input altogether.

This kind of ever-deepening strife could have led to divorce, but Cindy learned how to pray rather than fight. She asked the Lord to help her understand what was happening with Dan. She wanted to know why he was rejecting her when she was only trying to help. God revealed that Dan's diminished self-image had been learned from his father. He, too, had experienced that same kind of insecurity all of his life. Whatever the source of Dan's behavior, Cindy knew God had the power to change it.

She set herself to pray as long as it would take for God to break the bonds of self-loathing and mold her husband into *His* image. She asked God to help Dan find his identity in the Lord. She also prayed for God to enable her to speak to Dan in the Spirit and not in her flesh, so that her words would be received as encouragement to his soul rather than criticism.

It took a number of months before she saw any changes, but eventually there were major ones. First, Dan learned to trust that his wife was on the same team with him and not his opponent. They agreed to stop fighting and committed to work together. He started going to church more, and she could see he was praying and reading the Bible with new faith. He gradually began to see himself as one of God's much-loved sons and not an evolutionary mistake. The more he sensed his own worth and grew accepting of who he was, the more he was appreciated by everyone else. Not coincidentally, doors of opportunity began to open for him and Dan soon found the kind of acceptance and success he had always dreamed of having.

If your husband's self-image needs a makeover, be patient. The answers don't come overnight when a long-held pattern of thinking has to be broken. But you can appropriate the power of God to fight the enemy that feeds him familiar lies, so he can be free to hear God's truth. You'll find that as you intercede, God will reveal glimpses of the key to unlocking that particular thing in your husband. In other words, as you pray He'll show you *how* to pray.

I firmly believe that the tendency toward a midlife crisis can be hindered by praying along this same line. Any toxicity still in a man's soul after he reaches his fifties will eventually pour out of him like a poison. It's as if the invisible dam holding it back weakens with age. When it breaks, the flood can be strong enough to carry him away. Having his identity soundly established in the Lord will make a major difference in how he gets through that time.

God says our first steps are to be toward Him: seeking His face, following His laws, putting Him first and self-centered pursuits last. When we line up with Him, He leads the way and all we have to do is follow. As we look to Him, the glory of His image gets imprinted upon us. When our self-image gets so wrapped up in God that we lose ourselves in the process, we're free. We want that liberty for our husbands, as well as ourselves.

Your husband will never see who *he* really is until he sees who *God* really is. Pray that he finds his true identity.

Prayer

Lord, I pray that (husband's name) will find his identity in You. Help him to understand his worth through Your eyes and by Your standards. May he recognize the unique qualities You've placed in him and be able to appreciate them. Enable him to see himself the way You see him, understanding that "You have made him a little lower than the angels, and You crowned him with glory and honor. You have made him to have dominion over the works of Your hands; You have put all things under his feet" (Psalm 8:4-6). Quiet the voices that tell him otherwise and give him ears to hear Your voice telling him that it will not be his perfection that gets him through life successfully, it will be Yours.

Reveal to him that "he is the image and glory of God" (1 Corinthians 11:7), and he is "complete in Him, who is the head of all principality and power" (Colossians 2:10). Give him the peace and security of knowing that he is accepted, not rejected, by You. Free him from the self-focus and self-consciousness that can imprison his soul. Help him to see who *You* really are so he'll know who *he* really is. May his true self-image be the image of Christ stamped upon his soul.

POWER TOOLS

Whom He foreknew, He also predestined to be
conformed to the image of His Son, that He might
be the firstborn among many brethren.
ROMANS 8:29

We all, with unveiled face, beholding as in a mirror
the glory of the Lord, are being transformed into the
same image from glory to glory, just as by the Spirit
of the Lord.
2 CORINTHIANS 3:18

You have put off the old man with his deeds,
and have put on the new man who is
renewed in knowledge according
to the image of Him who
created him.
COLOSSIANS 3:9,10

If anyone is a hearer of the word and not a doer, he is
like a man observing his natural face in a mirror; for
he observes himself, goes away, and immediately forgets what kind of man he was. But he who looks into
the perfect law of liberty and continues in it, and is
not a forgetful hearer, but a doer of the work, this
one will be blessed in what he does.
JAMES 1:23-25

Arise, shine; for your light has come! And the
glory of the LORD is risen upon you.
ISAIAH 60:1

CHAPTER TWENTY-NINE

His Faith

I always smile when someone tells me he or she has no faith, because I know it's probably not true. Everyone lives by faith to a certain extent. When you go to a doctor, you need faith to trust his diagnosis. When the pharmacy fills your prescription, you have faith that you'll receive the appropriate medicine. When you eat at a restaurant, you trust that the people serving you have not contaminated or poisoned the food. (Some restaurants require more faith than others.) Every day is a walk of faith on some level. Everyone believes in something. "God has dealt to each one a measure of faith" (Romans 12:3).

We choose what we will believe in. Some people choose to believe in themselves, some in government, some in evil, some in science, some in the newspaper, some in hard work, some in other people, and some in God. The only person I have ever known who didn't believe in anything ended up in a mental hospital because it drove her crazy. Faith is something we can't live without.

Faith is something we can't *die* without either. Our faith determines what happens to us after we leave this world. If you have faith in Jesus, you know that your eternal future is secure. That's because "the Spirit of Him who raised Jesus from the dead . . . will also give life to your mortal bodies through His Spirit who dwells in you" (Romans 8:11). In other words, if the same Spirit who raised Jesus from the dead dwells in you, He will raise you up as well. Having certainty about what happens to us when we die will greatly affect how we live today. Confidence in our eternal future gives us a perspective on living in the present that is laced with confidence as well.

Here's a scary thought! When healing some blind men, Jesus said, "According to your faith let it be to you" (Matthew 9:29). Doesn't that make you want to reevaluate your level of trust in God? The good news is that this means we have a certain amount of control over our lives and can, to some extent, determine how things are going to turn out for us. Our lives don't have to be left up to chance, or allowed to go flapping in the breeze according to whatever wind is blowing at the moment. Our faith will help determine our outcome.

We all have times of doubt. Even Jesus wondered why God had forsaken Him. It wasn't that He doubted God's existence or ability to come to His rescue, He just didn't expect to feel forsaken. Sometimes we don't doubt God's existence, or whether He is *able* to help us, we just doubt His desire to have any immediate impact on our lives. *Surely He is too busy for my problems*, we think. But the truth is, He's not.

Does your husband have times of doubt? If so, your prayers for him to have ever-increasing faith will make a big difference in his life. Even if he doesn't know the Lord, you can still pray for faith to rise in his heart and look for an improvement in his level of peace. There is nothing in your husband's life that can't be conquered or positively affected with an added measure of faith in God. Jesus said of any man who has faith to believe in Him, "out of his heart will flow rivers of living water" (John 7:38). That alone can be enough to wash away a lifetime of pain, trouble, fear, sorrow, apathy, hopelessness, failure, and doubt. Shall we pray?

Prayer

Lord, I pray that You will give (husband's name) an added measure of faith today. Enlarge his ability to believe in You, Your Word, Your promises, Your ways, and Your power. Put a longing in His heart to talk with You and hear Your voice. Give him an understanding of what it means to bask in Your presence and not just ask for things. May he seek You, rely totally upon You, be led by You, put You first, and acknowledge You in everything he does.

Lord, You've said that "faith comes by hearing, and hearing by the word of God" (Romans 10:17). Feed his soul with Your Word so his faith grows big enough to believe that with You all things are possible (Matthew 19:26). Give him unfailing certainty that what You've promised to do, You will do (Romans 4:21). Make his faith a shield of protection. Put it into action to move the mountains in his life. Your Word says, "the just shall live by faith" (Romans 1:17); I pray that he will live the kind of faith-filled life You've called us all to experience. May he know with complete certainty "how great is Your goodness, which You have laid up for those who fear You, which You have prepared for those who trust in You" (Psalm 31:19).

POWER TOOLS

Let him ask in faith, with no doubting, for he who
doubts is like a wave of the sea driven and tossed by
the wind. For let not that man suppose that he will
receive anything from the Lord; he is a double-
minded man, unstable in all his ways.
JAMES 1:6-8

Whatever is not from faith is sin.
ROMANS 14:23

If you have faith as a mustard seed, you will say to
this mountain, "Move from here to there," and it will
move; and nothing will be impossible for you.
MATTHEW 17:20

I have been crucified with Christ; it is no longer I
who live, but Christ lives in me; and the life which I
now live in the flesh I live by faith in the Son of
God, who loved me and gave Himself for me.
GALATIANS 2:20

Therefore, having been justified by faith, we have
peace with God through our Lord Jesus Christ.
ROMANS 5:1

CHAPTER THIRTY

His Future

*N*one of us can live without a vision for our future. If we don't have one, we flounder aimlessly. Without it, life seems pointless and we die a little every day. "Where there is no vision, the people perish" (Proverbs 29:18 KJV).

Having a vision doesn't necessarily mean knowing the specifics about what is going to happen next. It has to do with sensing the general direction you're moving in and having hope that something good is on the horizon. It's knowing that you *do* have a future and a purpose, and that it is bright.

Not every man has that certainty. When he doesn't, you can almost see life draining from him. Even the ones who do, don't necessarily have it all the time. Even the most spiritual man can get overtired, burned out, beaten down, distanced from God, confused about who he is and why he is here, and lose his vision for the future. He can misplace his sense of purpose and become overwhelmed and hopeless because of it. If he loses sight of his dreams and forgets the truth about himself and his situation, he can end up believing destructive lies about his future. "My people are destroyed for lack of knowledge" (Hosea 4:6).

God says not to listen to voices that speak lies, for "they speak a vision of their own heart, not from the mouth of the LORD" (Jeremiah 23:16). Any vision for the future that is full of failure and empty of hope is not from God (Jeremiah 29:11). But God can restore vision where it has been lost. He can give hope to dream again. He can bring His truth to bear upon the lies of discouragement. He can give assurance of a promising future. Prayer is the avenue through which He can accomplish it.

My husband said that one of the times my prayers meant the most to him was when we moved from Los Angeles to Nashville. It was very hard for all of us to leave the people we loved and start over again. There was so much at stake and it was a difficult transition, not to mention a big step of faith. We didn't know how it would all work out, but we moved in certainty that we were following God's leading. We trusted that our lives were safe in His hands. My prayer for Michael during that season was that he not lose the vision God had given him for the future. When circumstances caused him to temporarily lose his spiritual sight, he said my prayers were instrumental in restoring it.

We have to remember that Father God has drawn up His will. His estate is divided equally among His children. All that *He* has, *we* will have. We are "heirs of God and joint heirs with Christ" (Romans 8:17). I've read my copy of the will and it says we don't have any idea of all God has for us, because He has more for us than we ever imagined. "Eye has not seen, nor ear heard, nor have entered into the heart of man the things which God has prepared for those who love Him" (1 Corinthians 2:9). It promises that "the blameless will inherit good" (Proverbs 28:10). It says that not only will we have everything we need in *this* life, but the most significant portion of it will be ours after we die. Then we will be with Him and we will want nothing more.

If your husband's eyes get so focused on the day-to-day details of living that he loses his vision for the future, your prayers can lift his sights. They can help him see that God is his future and he needs to run his life in a way that invests in that. "Do you not know that those who run in a race all run, but one receives the prize? Run in such a way that you may obtain it" (1 Corinthians 9:24). You don't want your husband to be a man who speaks a vision of his own heart and loses the prize. You want him to be able to see from God's perspective.

God doesn't want us to know the future, He wants us to know *Him*. He wants us to trust Him to guide us into the future one step at a time. In order to understand God's leading, we must seek Him for every step. "Those who seek the LORD understand all" (Proverbs 28:5). We must also stay close enough to hear His answer. The Lord is the giver of vision; pray that your husband looks to Him for it. With God, his future is secure.

Prayer

Lord, I pray that You would give (husband's name) a vision for his future. Help him to understand that Your plans for him are for good and not evil—to give him a future and a hope (Jeremiah 29:11). Fill him with the knowledge of Your will in all wisdom and spiritual understanding; that he may have a walk worthy of You, fully pleasing You, being fruitful in every good work and increasing in the knowledge of

You (Colossians 1:9,10). May he live with leading from the Holy Spirit and not walk in doubt and fear of what may happen. Help him to mature and grow in You daily, submitting to You all his dreams and desires, knowing that "the things which are impossible with men are possible with God" (Luke 18:27). Give him God-ordained goals and show him how to conduct himself in a way that always invests in his future.

I pray that he will be active in service for You all the days of his life. Keep him from losing his sense of purpose and fill him with hope for his future as an "anchor of the soul, both sure and steadfast" (Hebrews 6:19). Give him "his heart's desire" (Psalm 21:2) and "the heritage of those who fear Your name" (Psalm 61:5). Plant him firmly in Your house and keep him fresh and flourishing and bearing fruit into old age (Psalm 92:13,14). And when it comes time for him to leave this earth and go to be with You, may he have such a strong vision for his eternal future that it makes his transition smooth, painless, and accompanied by peace and joy. Until that day, I pray he will find the vision for his future in You.

POWER TOOLS

I know the thoughts that I think toward you,
says the LORD, thoughts of peace and not of evil,
to give you a future and a hope.
JEREMIAH 29:11

Mark the blameless man, and observe the upright; for
the future of that man is peace. But the
transgressors shall be destroyed together;
the future of the wicked shall be cut off.
PSALM 37:37,38

Those who are planted in the house of the LORD
shall flourish in the courts of our God. They shall
still bear fruit in old age; they shall be fresh and
flourishing, to declare that the LORD is upright; He is
my rock, and there is no unrighteousness in Him.
PSALM 92:13-15

One thing I have desired of the LORD, that will I
seek: that I may dwell in the house of the LORD all
the days of my life, to behold the beauty of the LORD,
and to inquire in His temple.
PSALM 27:4

There is hope in your future.
JEREMIAH 31:17

Other Books
by Stormie Omartian

The Power of a Praying® Husband
The Power of a Praying® Husband
The Power of a Praying® Husband Prayer & Study Guide
The Power of a Praying® Husband Book of Prayers

The Power of a Praying® Parent
The Power of a Praying® Parent
The Power of a Praying® Parent Prayer and Study Guide
The Power of a Praying® Parent Book of Prayers

The Power of a Praying® Wife
The Power of a Praying® Wife
The Power of a Praying® Wife Prayer and Study Guide
The Power of a Praying® Wife Audio
The Power of a Praying® Wife Book of Prayers

The Power of a Praying® Woman
The Power of a Praying® Woman
The Power of a Praying® Woman Prayer and Study Guide
The Power of a Praying® Woman Book of Prayers

The Power of Praying® Together
The Power of Praying® Together

The Prayer That Changes Everything™
The Prayer That Changes Everything™
The Prayer That Changes Everything™ Book of Prayers

Just Enough Light for the Step I'm On
Just Enough Light for the Step I'm On
Just Enough Light for the Step I'm On Book of Prayers
Just Enough Light for the Step I'm On—A Devotional
Prayer Journey

Other Items
Greater Health God's Way
Book of Prayer
Stormie
The Power of Praying®
The Power of a Praying® Teen
The Power of a Praying® Kid
The Power of a Praying® Woman Bible
Prayers for Emotional Wholeness